Those Who Walked by Faith
Trusting the Invisible Promises of God

A Bible Study Workbook by
Matthew Allen

© 2023 Spiritbuilding Publishers.
All rights reserved. No part of this book may be reproduced in any form without the written permission of the publisher.

Published by
Spiritbuilding Publishers
9700 Ferry Road, Waynesville, Ohio 45068

THOSE WHO WALKED BY FAITH
Trusting the Invisible Promises of God
By Matthew Allen

All Scripture references are taken from Holman Bible Publishers' *Christian Standard Bible* unless otherwise noted.

ISBN: 978-1955285-81-0

Spiritbuilding
PUBLISHERS

spiritbuilding.com

Table of Contents

Why This Study? 1

Lesson 1   He Still Speaks: Abel 3
What Abel's Faith Led Him to Do

Lesson 2   He Walked with God: Enoch 11
Prioritizing Your Relationship with God

Lesson 3   He Found Grace: Noah 20
Unwavering Trust in the Promises of God

Lesson 4   A Friend with God: Abraham 29
True Faith and Devotion to God

Lesson 5   Trusting God's Promises: The Faith of the Patriarchs 40
The Legacy of Unwavering Faith

Lesson 6   Looking to the Reward: Moses 49
Making the Faithful Choice

Lesson 7   Courageous Leadership: Joshua 58
A Bold, Obedient Faith

Lesson 8   Harlot to Heroine: Rahab 69
Great Faith Leads to Great Deliverance

Lesson 9   Faith to Follow Through: Gideon 76
From Fear to Faith

Lesson 10   A Woman Who Changed History: Hannah 84
Discovering the Power of Prayer

Lesson 11   A Man After God's Own Heart: David 91
Trusting God's Guidance in Life's Challenges

Lesson 12   Israel's Great Prophet: Elijah 99
Faith Lived Out

Lesson 13   For a Time Like This: Esther 107
Trusting in God's Providence

Why This Study?

Throughout Scripture, we find that faith, as described in Hebrews 11:1, is more than simple belief—it is an active trust in the future God has assured us. It is not just an intellectual assent to the promises laid out in the Bible but an embracing of them in their full glory and detail. Faith perseveres through life's trials, holding steadfast to a vision of eternity with God, where the pains of the present are but a memory. The heroes of faith listed in Hebrews 11, each faced formidable challenges. Yet, they did not allow these difficulties to hinder their progress or dim their vision; they pressed on and received commendation from God.

God calls upon us, as He did them, to trust in a future He has written—one of ultimate blessing and eternal joy. Hebrews 10:38 underscores the necessity of this faith—we must not *shrink back* but must keep moving forward. God takes no pleasure in those who withdraw in doubt. Hebrews 10:39 further warns that to draw back is to embrace destruction. Yet, Hebrews 11 is there to encourage us by reminding us of those who lived by faith and did amazing things despite not receiving what had been promised in their lifetime. They trusted in its eventual fulfillment, living with a faith that was as real to them as the tangible world around them.

Faith, therefore, is not simply hoping for the best; *it is the assurance of things hoped for, the conviction of things not seen*, as stated in Hebrews 11:1. It is a tangible trust in the invisible promises of God. It is possessing the substance of what we await with anticipation, the essence of our future hope.

Concerning the Bible characters you will study in this workbook, the promises of God were so real to them that they built their entire lives around them, trusting in what they had not yet seen or experienced. Just as they did, 2000 years after the cross, we, too, trust in the promises of Scripture. We believe in heaven, in eternal life, in a future with God—all unseen, yet real to us. This belief creates a present reality as we trust in what is to come, shaping how we live now. It informs our worship, our observance of the Lord's Supper, and it undergirds every aspect of our lives. Our faith is the conviction of things not seen, the evidence of our hope, moving us to live in anticipation of God's future revelation.

Romans 8:24–26 speaks of being saved by hope, a hope that is patient and unwavering because it is rooted in faith. This faith provides a present substance to our hope, steadying us in our earthly pilgrimage as we look for that "better country"—a heavenly one. Without faith, Hebrews 11.6 tells us, we have nothing. Life without God is devoid of hope, but in faith, we find a saving hope, a firm foundation for both the present and the future.

I'm excited you have decided to explore the heroes of faith in this workbook. Let the testimony of these saints inspire you to embrace the hope that only faith in God can provide.

Matthew Allen

November 2023

Lesson 1

He Still Speaks: Abel
What Abel's Faith Led Him to Do

Read

Hebrews 11.4

Genesis 4.1–12

Introduction

Someone once said death is never the last word in the life of a righteous man. When we depart this life, we all leave something behind. Our legacy will either be as a blossom of beauty, or something that spreads like a cancer. Just make a quick comparison between the legacies of Paul and Nero. Think of two individuals closer to modern times: Hitler and Churchill. Dead men do tell tales. They are not silent. They loudly speak. Notice what was said about Abel in Hebrews 11.4:

> And through his faith, though he died, he still speaks.

Who was Abel? What does he say to Christians today? How is he someone who walked by faith? Abel has been rightly called the first man of faith. Born outside of Eden, he never had the opportunity to know God in the same way his parents did. He was the first man to really exercise positive faith in God. He not only believed, but he also bet his life on it.

In this lesson, we will examine Hebrews 11.4 in depth.

> By faith Abel offered to God a more acceptable sacrifice than Cain, through which he was commended as righteous, God commending him by accepting his gifts. And through his faith, though he died, he still speaks.

Abel's faith led him to do three things. First, it moved him to ***offer a more acceptable sacrifice***. Secondly, it led him to be ***commended as righteous***. And last, it enabled him to ***speak***, though he is dead.

A More Acceptable Sacrifice

In the opening verses of Genesis 4, we read of the birth of Cain and Abel. Cain grew up to be a tiller of the ground and Abel grew up to be a keeper of sheep, 4.2. The next two verses are extremely important:

> In the course of time Cain presented some of the land's produce as an offering to the Lord. And Abel also presented an offering— some of the firstborn of his flock and their fat portions. The Lord had regard for Abel and his offering, Genesis 4.3–4.

While the details remain undisclosed, the verses suggest at some point God must have set in place some initial expectations for worship. First, a designated spot existed for worshiping God. As evident from the verses, both individuals presented their offerings to the Lord. Presumably, an altar stood at this site. Who informed them of this worship spot? And who introduced the concept of an altar? Additionally, there was a specific time designated for worship. In its original form, the term "the course of time" translates to "at the end of days." This implies that they were expected to offer their sacrifices at a specified time. God must have designated a particular day for these offerings. It's noteworthy that both approached simultaneously, hinting that they both were aware of the timing. Cain and Abel come at the same time and location but with distinct gifts. Only one offering was accepted by God, suggesting God had set certain guidelines.

Following their expulsion from the garden, it's plausible that God would have instructed Adam and Eve about the proper time and place for worship and the appropriate mode of sacrifice. Hebrews 11.4 mentions Abel's sacrifice was made in *faith*. But where does faith originate? As Romans 10.17 puts it, "faith comes from what is heard, and what is heard comes through the message about Christ." We can't believe in the unknown. Given Abel's faithful sacrifice, it's likely he understood God's wishes, believed in them, and acted accordingly. By comprehending that a sacrifice was necessary because of sin, he manifested his faith through action. Abel's obedience and recognition of his flaws starkly contrasted with Cain's non-compliance and denial of his sins. Perhaps, after the events in the garden, God relayed the solution to human sinfulness. This communication might resemble the verses we've received:

- "without the shedding of blood there is no forgiveness," Hebrews 9.22.
- "For the life of a creature is in the blood … it is the lifeblood that makes atonement," Leviticus 17.11.

Abel was prepared for this sacrifice. Genesis 4.4 implies he had already prepared the animals by separating their fat. He acted with surety. Abel believed God and that faith motivated him to approach God in the prescribed manner. It was as if he was saying:

> "God, this is what You said You wanted and You said if I brought it, You would forgive my sin. I brought it. I believe You God. I acknowledge my sin. I acknowledge the prescribed remedy."

Cain would have had the same information. Instead, he brought only what was convenient for him and did his own thing. Cain did not believe God and thought he could approach God by his own works. He was steadfastly rejected. Cain has been called the father of false religion. He tried to come to God by another way. He failed. False religion is an invented way to God. *There is a way that seems right to a person, but its end is the way to death,* Proverbs 14.12.

Abel's way to God was based on something he was told. God's righteousness is not arbitrary. It is based on obedience to a prescribed plan. Abel was righteous. Cain was not. Consider 1 John 3.11–12:

> For this is the message you have heard from the beginning: We should love one another, unlike Cain, who was of the evil one and murdered his brother. And why did he murder him? Because his deeds were evil, and his brother's were righteous.

To disobey is evil. To obey is righteous. God gave them what He wanted and they either obeyed it or they didn't.

There is one last consideration we need to make with Abel's offering. Genesis 4 says he brought of the *firstlings* of his flock. **He gave his best**. Compare that to Cain, who just brought of the fruit of the ground. Because of all these things, Abel brought *by faith* **a more acceptable sacrifice**.

Abel Obtained Righteousness

Regarding their offerings we are told, *The Lord had regard for Abel and his offering, but he did not have regard for Cain and his offering,* Genesis 4.4b–5a. The only thing that obtained righteousness for Abel was that he did what God told him. Cain didn't. That's the only difference. A faith that responds is the only thing that changes a persons' relationship with God. It is not about *how good we are*. It is not about whether you are better or worse than anyone else. It's that you came to God on the terms that He established. That's all he asks. Abel was as much a sinner as Cain, but he believed God and obeyed. Because of that faith, it was counted to Abel for righteousness.

True faith is always obedient. Jesus told those who believed on Him, *Then Jesus said to the Jews who had believed him, "If you continue in my word, you really are my disciples. You will know the truth, and the truth will set you free,"* John 8.31–32. God honored Abel because his faith was alive. It was alive in the way he obeyed. The teaching of James 2.14–26 goes right along with this. Our faith is alive when it manifests itself by action. We can't work to get to God, but having come to Him, our works will become evidence of our faith. We have been *called unto good works,* Ephesians 2.10.

Abel, Being Dead, Still Speaks

Genesis 4 says God gave Cain another opportunity to do right.

> Cain was furious, and he looked despondent. Then the Lord said to Cain, "Why are you furious? And why do you look despondent? If you do what is right, won't you be accepted? But if you do not do what is right, sin is crouching at the door. Its desire is for you, but you must rule over it." Cain said to his brother Abel, "Let's go out to the field." And while they were in the field, Cain attacked his brother Abel and killed him, Genesis 4.5b–8.

Instead, Cain chose to do evil and kill his brother. Note how God confronts Cain in the aftermath.

How does Abel speak?

First, Abel spoke to Cain. After his death, God said,

Then he said, "What have you done? Your brother's blood cries out to me from the ground! So now you are cursed, alienated from the ground that opened its mouth to receive your brother's blood you have shed. If you work the ground, it will never again give you its yield. You will be a restless wanderer on the earth," Genesis 4.10–12.

Wherever Cain went, his crops would struggle. He would spend the rest of his life walking on the soil that represented the blood of his brother— *always unyielding.* Abel, even though he was dead, continued to speak for the remainder of the life of Cain.

But Abel still speaks today. He speaks that sin will be severely punished for the one who does not live in obedience to God. We cannot expect to make up our own religion and system of works to be pleasing of God. We must follow God's pattern by faith. Only then will He bless us.

What's in This for Us?

Legacy Matters

The choices we make in life have a lasting impact, even after we're gone. Strive to leave a positive legacy that uplifts and inspires.

Genuine Faith Matters

Just like Abel, genuine faith requires action and isn't just a mental acknowledgement. Our beliefs should drive our behavior.

Follow God's Instructions

God has provided guidelines for worship and obedience. Trusting and adhering to these guidelines showcases true faith.

Understanding Leads to Obedience

Knowledge of what God desires, like Abel had, can lead to actions that are in line with God's wishes. Abel's obedience to God's commands resulted in blessings, whereas Cain's disobedience led to negative outcomes. This highlights the significance of adhering to divine guidance.

Faith and Righteousness are Linked

Abel's sacrifice was accepted because it was done with understanding and faith. In contrast, Cain's sacrifice was rejected because it wasn't what God asked for. This emphasizes the importance of aligning actions with genuine faith. Abel's obedience to God's instructions made him righteous. Obedience to God's commands is a testament to one's faith. Faith isn't just about belief; it's about how those beliefs translate into actions.

The Danger of Jealousy

Cain's jealousy led him down a destructive path. Recognizing and managing negative emotions can prevent harmful actions.

Conclusion

The story of Abel serves as a powerful lesson for every Christian. Through his unwavering faith and obedience, he set a precedent for all who seek to truly follow God's commands. In contrast, Cain's disobedience, and refusal to offer what was required by God not only led to his downfall but stands as a warning for those who choose to go their own way instead of adhering to the path laid down by God.

For Class Interaction and Discussion

Lesson Outline
1. **Introduction:**
    —Legacy of a righteous man
    —Examples: Paul and Nero, Hitler, and Churchill
    —Legacy of Abel: Hebrews 11.4
2. **Background of Abel:**
    —Born outside of Eden
    —Relationship with God
    —Importance of positive faith
3. **Understanding Abel's Sacrifice:**
    —Cain and Abel's offerings
    —God's guidelines on worship
    —The significance of Abel's faith
4. **Abel Obtained Righteousness:**
    —Genesis 4.4b–5a
    —Significance of obedient faith
    —Difference between Abel and Cain's faith
5. **Abel, Being Dead, Still Speaks:**
    —Cain's choice and its consequences
    —Abel's continuous influence
    —Abel's message today
6. **What's in This for Us?**
    —Importance of legacy
    —Power of genuine faith

Thought Questions for Discussion

1. How does the legacy of a righteous person differ from one that isn't righteous? Can you think of modern examples?

2. How did Abel demonstrate his faith in God differently from Cain?

3. What do you think the specific guidelines for worship were, given to Cain and Abel?

4. How does obedience play a role in faith? How is it different from just believing?

5. In what ways does Abel's story emphasize the importance of following God's prescribed way of worship?

6. How does Abel's sacrifice resonate with modern-day Christians? How can we apply the lessons from his life to ours?

7. In what ways do our choices today create a legacy for tomorrow?

8. How do our actions and choices today serve as a testimony to our faith?

Group Activity

Legacy Mapping: On a piece of paper, jot down:
1. One positive action or choice you made in the past that has had lasting effects.
2. One negative action or choice you made and its long-term consequences.
3. One action or choice you can make today to positively influence your legacy.

Scripture Dive: Read the following passages: John 8.31–32; James 2.14–26; and Ephesians 2.10. Discuss how true faith is always obedient.

Walking with God Today

Reflect on your own offerings to God during the upcoming week. Are you giving Him the best in every area of your life, or are there areas where you've been holding back? Journal your reflections.

Lesson 2

He Walked with God: Enoch

Prioritizing Your Relationship with God

Read

Hebrews 11.5–6

Genesis 5.21–24

Jude 14–15

Introduction

In his hall of fame of faith, the Hebrew writer devotes two verses to Enoch. That is a sizable amount of text when we consider the overall Biblical record. We read:

> By faith Enoch was taken up so that he should not see death, and he was not found, because God had taken him. Now before he was taken he was commended as having pleased God. And without faith it is impossible to please him, for whoever would draw near to God must believe that he exists and that he rewards those who seek him, Hebrews 11.5–6.

Remember, when we read the book of Hebrews, we are reading a letter addressed to Christians struggling in their faith, 10.35–39. Now they are being encouraged to press on, emboldened by their unabated access to God and His love for them. By directing their minds back to each Bible hero in chapter 11, the writer hoped to spurn his readers into a more energetic and fulfilling relationship with Christ.

Previously, we discussed the life of Abel. Cain and Abel must have both been instructed on what God's expectations for sacrifice were. By faith, Abel responded to God's instructions and trusted that his sins would be forgiven. God communicated his terms of pardon and Abel trusted in God through his obedience.

Isn't it the same for us today?

God has revealed His terms of pardon, and we demonstrate our trust in Him by our obedience to the gospel. If Abel shows us how to get started in this relationship with God, then Enoch shows us the importance of walking with God daily.

The Old Testament Connection

In the Old Testament, Enoch is mentioned in Genesis 5. This chapter is a collection of genealogy tracing the line of descendants from Seth. Over the course of the first twenty verses, we read about some individuals who had incredible life spans. Enoch's father, Jared, lived 962 years! Jared, just like all the ones before him, died. But something is strikingly different with Enoch. Notice:

> Enoch was 65 years old when he fathered Methuselah. And after he fathered Methuselah, Enoch walked with God 300 years and fathered other sons and daughters. So Enoch's life lasted 365 years. Enoch walked with God; then he was not there because God took him, Genesis 5.21–24.

Unlike those before him, Enoch did not die. Both Hebrews 11 and this passage simply say *God took him.*

It is also interesting to note that Enoch's son, Methuselah, lived 969 years! This is the longest lifespan recorded in the Bible. In Hebrew, Methuselah's name means, "Man of the sending forth," or "man shot out." From his very beginning, God used him to warn the generations of the upcoming judgment in the great flood. Methuselah died in the year of the flood. Enoch also warned people of upcoming judgment. See Jude 14–15.

Genesis 5.22 says that for the 300 years after fathering Methuselah, Enoch *walked with God.* 300 years is an incredible amount of time. We experience struggles in our relationship with God over our short lifespan. Can you imagine sustaining that for three centuries? Also, keep in mind that the world around Enoch was getting worse continually. Yet, he remained true and steadfast to the Almighty God. He was in daily, intimate communion with God. Our text in Hebrews says *he was commended as having pleased God*, 11.5. Like Abel, he must have been a man who recognized his sin and acknowledged the need for sacrifice. He would have trusted in God in the truest and purest sense for his salvation, his forgiveness, and his life.

Enoch is not the only character during the patriarchal period who walked with God. The Biblical record tells us Noah *walked* with God, Genesis 6.6–8. Abraham was called to *walk* with God, Genesis 17.1. Later, Abraham spoke of how he had *walked* with God, Genesis 24.40. Finally, the term is used once more in Genesis 48.15.

What does it mean to walk with God? It refers to *step-by-step fellowship or daily communion*. This is what is involved in salvation. Because Noah walked with God, he escaped judgment. Because Abraham walked with God, he received blessing. Because Enoch walked with God, he escaped death. Enoch is the illustration of salvation's great promise. That is, eternal life in heaven. We have been promised that we will be delivered from our world of sin, decay, disease, and death and enter the presence of the Lord.

Genesis 5.24 puts it this way, *Enoch walked with God, and he was not, for God took him*. In the original language, the phrase *took him* describes a sudden, inexplicable disappearance. One day during his 365th year, he was gone. He disappeared. Enoch was a model of faith that walked with God, being rewarded with eternal life.

The Hebrews Account

The Hebrew writer connects the story of Enoch with the definition of faith. Enoch was *commended as having pleased God*, and then we are told, **without faith it is impossible to please him** … Hebrews 11.5b–6a. The beginning of any relationship with God starts with faith. This (faith) is the basis upon which we approach God. Enoch depended on God. He put his trust in Him and thus was reconciled to and received by God. What does it mean to put your faith in Him?

The answer is seen in the second part of Hebrews 11.6: *since the one who draws near to him must believe that he exists*. The New American Standard translates this part of the passage this way: *for he who comes to God must believe that He is*.

This is not just as simple as saying there is a God, or professing belief in God and being "spiritual." Rather, it is an acknowledgment that HE is who HE is, the only true God. God is not just one of many gods. He is THE God. The basis of faith begins with this recognition. So, how do we know the God who is God? Simply put, we know Him by virtue of His revelation. Throughout human history, God has revealed Himself again and again. He has revealed Himself through His creation and ultimately through the Scripture. Enoch believed in the true God as He had revealed Himself. God is a God of holiness and righteousness, a God who hates sin. These things would have been eminently clear to Enoch.

But not only did Enoch believe that God is who He is, He also believed that He is a rewarder of those who seek Him, Hebrews 11.6c. Enoch believed that God rewards those who pursue Him. He believed that God was a personal, forgiving, loving, gracious God who would provide salvation to those who know Him. He believed in a personal, caring God who wanted to be reconciled to him in a personal way. Enoch knew He was a loving God with whom he could fellowship and to whom he could be restored.

This has always been the basis for a relationship with God. As he prepared to die, David said to his son, Solomon:

> As for you, my son Solomon, know the God of your father, and serve Him with a whole heart and a willing mind; for the LORD searches all hearts, and understands every intent of the thoughts. If you seek Him, He will let you find Him; but if you forsake Him, He will reject you forever, 1 Chronicles 28.9.

In Psalm 119:10, David said, *with all my heart, I have sought you.* In Proverbs 8:17 God said, *I love those who love me; and those who diligently seek me will find me.* And finally, Jeremiah 29:13, contains a wonderful promise: *You will seek Me and find Me when you search for Me with all your heart.* Each of these passages should tell us something about God. He is a Savior. He desires to rescue us from sin. He wants a relationship with us.

Take a few moments to read the following passages that can give you hope for today:

- John 3.16–17.
- Ephesians 1.3–8.
- Colossians 1.12–14.

God is a lavish rewarder of those who come on His terms. He grants forgiveness and gives us a new heart. He blesses us with the Holy Spirit, eternal life, mercy, grace, peace, joy, love, heaven, power over evil, it's all there. What a wonderful blessing and privilege it is to walk with God.

Jude and Enoch

In just two short verses, Enoch is mentioned in Jude's epistle. It gives us insight as to what Enoch was doing during those 365 years of his life.

> It was about these that Enoch, in the seventh generation from Adam, prophesied: "Look! The Lord comes with tens of thousands of his holy ones to execute judgment on all and to convict all the ungodly

concerning all the ungodly acts that they have done in an ungodly way, and concerning all the harsh things ungodly sinners have said against him", Jude 14–15.

There must have been false teachers in his day who served as agents of Satan—promoting his agenda. Enoch stood up to these influences. While he walked with God, he preached and warned those of his day of the upcoming judgment of God. He was busy urging others to prepare!

Isn't that our job as Christians?

We serve others by encouraging them to know and understand the only way to escape God's final judgment is to cease from sin and enter a relationship with Him. There is no other way! Jesus said, *I am the way, the truth, and the life. No one comes to the Father but by Me,* John 14.6. We need to be busy warning others of impending judgment, beseeching them to obey the gospel, and standing up against the cultural rot of our day. When the opportunities present themselves, we can tactfully point out the reality of the ultimate end of darkness: hell. It is not just a fairy tale.

The devil is not our friend. Those who walk with God see things from their proper perspective and understand the need to share with others the awful consequences of not having a relationship with God.

What's In This for Us?

Prioritize Daily Fellowship with God

Just as Enoch walked with God daily, we too should cultivate a consistent relationship with God. This can be achieved through daily prayer, scripture reading, and meditative reflection.

Faith is Essential

Remember that without faith, it's impossible to please God, Hebrews 11.6. Our belief isn't just about acknowledging God's existence but genuinely trusting Him in all circumstances.

God Rewards the Faithful

Enoch's life demonstrates that God acknowledges and rewards those who seek Him earnestly. Let's be encouraged that our faithfulness will not go unnoticed.

Be an Example in a Wayward World

Even as the world around Enoch spiraled into moral decay, he remained steadfast in his faith. We can be beacons of light in our world by living according to God's standards, no matter the prevailing culture around us.

Proclaim the Truth

Enoch didn't shy away from speaking about the upcoming judgment. We should be emboldened to share the gospel truth with others, warning them lovingly about the consequences of turning away from God.

Seek Him Wholeheartedly

A relationship with God requires a heart that seeks Him earnestly. David and Solomon knew this. We should commit to seeking God with all our heart, mind, and strength.

Embrace God's Promises

Scripture provides numerous assurances of God's love, protection, and rewards. Whenever we feel discouraged or lost, delving into these promises can provide comfort and direction.

Stand Against False Teaching

Just as Enoch stood against false teaching in his day, we should be equipped to discern and refute incorrect teaching and beliefs that stray from the scripture.

Serve Others by Sharing the Gospel

Enoch's life was not just about his personal walk with God but also about urging others to prepare for the coming judgment. We too should be active in sharing the gospel and guiding others toward a relationship with God.

Remember God's Lavish Rewards

God's blessings are numerous—from forgiveness to eternal life. Even in our daily struggles, remembering these rewards can give us hope and purpose.

Conclusion

Enoch's life serves as a testament to the rewards of a deep, consistent relationship with God. Despite living in challenging times, his faith never wavered. His story reminds us of the importance of faith, the need to prioritize our relationship with God, and the responsibility we have towards others. As we go about our daily lives, let's strive to walk with God just as Enoch did.

For Class Interaction and Discussion

Lesson Outline

1. **Introduction:**
   —Enoch's place in the Hebrew Hall of Fame

   —Context of Hebrews: Christians struggling in their faith

2. **Old Testament Connection:**

   —The significance of Enoch in the Old Testament

   —Enoch's unique relationship with God: He did not experience death

3. **The Hebrews Account:**

   —Defining faith

   —Approaching God with the right mindset

4. **Jude and Enoch:**

   —Enoch's role as mentioned in Jude's epistle

   —The responsibilities and roles Enoch played in his lifetime

Thought Questions for Discussion

1. Why do you think the Hebrew writer dedicated two verses to Enoch in particular?

2. In what ways do we, today, struggle with our faith like the Christians addressed in Hebrews?

3. What stands out to you about the way Enoch's story is told in Genesis 5?

4. How do you interpret the phrase, "Enoch walked with God; then he was not there because God took him"?

5. How do you define faith in your own life?

6. What does it mean to truly believe that God "is who He is"?

7. How does God reveal Himself to us today?

8. What can we infer about Enoch's life based on Jude 14–15?

9. Today, how can we be like Enoch and stand up to false teachings or influences?

Group Activity

Group Discussion: Divide into groups and discuss Enoch's steadfastness and daily communion with God in a world that was continuously deteriorating. What can we learn from this?

Scripture Dive: Examine the provided passages: John 3.16–17, Ephesians 1.3–8, Colossians 1.12–14. Discuss the promises of God and how they apply to our lives.

Walking with God Today

Reflect on your personal relationship with God. Consider how you can better "walk" with Him daily. Share one commitment you're willing to make this week to strengthen that walk.

Lesson 3

He Found Grace: Noah

Unwavering Trust in the Promises of God

Read
Hebrews 11.7

Genesis 6–7

Introduction

Noah's story is one of faith, obedience, and divine grace. He is commended as a righteous man in a time of widespread corruption and sin. Speaking of him, the Hebrew writer forever sealed his legacy when he wrote:

> By faith Noah, being warned by God concerning events as yet unseen, in reverent fear constructed an ark for the saving of his household. By this he condemned the world and became an heir of the righteousness that comes by faith, Hebrews 11.7.

Here the faith of Noah is highlighted, a faith that stood firm even when faced with the unimaginable task of building an ark to save his family from a flood—not just any flood—but a flood that would wipe out the entirety of mankind. Noah's story is not just a historical account; it is a divinely preserved story that speaks loudly about the nature of faith, obedience, and the grace of God.

As we examine the life of Noah, we will uncover the characteristics that set him apart in a generation that had turned its back on God. We will explore how his faith and obedience became a beacon of light in a dark time, and how his life exemplifies the power of God's grace. Noah found favor in the eyes of the Lord, not because he was perfect, but because he walked with God in faith and reverence.

This lesson aims to inspire and challenge us to examine our own lives considering Noah's example. How can we, like Noah, find grace in the eyes of the Lord? How does faith shape our response to God's warnings and instructions, even when they seem daunting or unclear?

God's Commands are Always Given in the Context of Grace

Genesis 6.5 paints a grim picture of the human condition, describing a world steeped in sin and rebellion against God.

> The LORD saw that human wickedness was widespread on the earth and that every inclination of the human mind was nothing but evil all the time.

The verse describes the ultimate progression of sin, where wickedness and corruption have completely taken over, leaving no room for righteousness or goodness. In verses 6–7, we see God's response to this depravity.

> The Lord regretted that he had made man on the earth, and he was deeply grieved. Then the Lord said, "I will wipe mankind, whom I created, off the face of the earth, together with the animals, creatures that crawl, and birds of the sky—for I regret that I made them."

God was grieved by the sinfulness of mankind and decides to bring an end to humanity, except for Noah and his family. This decision reflects God's holy and just nature, as He cannot tolerate sin and must act against it. However, against this backdrop of judgment, we discover a glimmer of hope.

> Noah, however, found favor with the Lord, Genesis 6.8.

Here is a righteous man in a corrupt generation. Don't quickly pass over the meaning of the word *found* in this verse. It implies an active pursuit on Noah's part. He was actively seeking God, striving to live a life of righteousness amidst a sinful world. This does not mean that Noah was without sin, as he, like all humans, was affected by the fall. However, he dealt with his sin, repented, and found grace in the eyes of the Lord. His life was marked by faith, and as a result, God regarded him as guiltless and not liable for sin and wrongdoing.

Genesis 6.9 further reveals Noah's character, describing him as a righteous man, blameless among the people of his time, and one who walked with God.

> These are the family records of Noah. Noah was a righteous man, blameless among his contemporaries; Noah walked with God.

These attributes highlight the close relationship Noah had with God, marked by obedience, faithfulness, and a commitment to respect God's ways. It is important for us to recognize that God's instructions and commands are always given in the context of grace. Even amid judgment, God provides a way of salvation and redemption for those who seek Him and live by faith. Noah's story is a powerful example of this truth, reminding us that God's grace is available to all who earnestly seek Him, regardless of the sinfulness that surrounds us.

How God Communicated with Noah

In Genesis 6.13, God initiated communication with Noah, delivering a warning that judgment and destruction were imminent. The very future of mankind hung in the balance, and God chose Noah to play a crucial role in preserving life on earth. This moment highlights the severity of the situation, as God reveals the extent of human wickedness and His decision to cleanse the world through the flood. Noah, standing as a righteous man in a corrupt generation, was chosen to bear the weight of this revelation. God's communication was clear and direct, leaving no room for misunderstanding the urgency and gravity of the situation.

Following the warning, God provided Noah with specific instructions and commands in Genesis 6.14. He was to build an ark, which would serve as a sanctuary for him, his family, and representatives of every living creature. The purpose was clear: the preservation of mankind. God's instructions were detailed and precise, ensuring that Noah had everything he needed to fulfill this divine mandate. This moment underscores God's providential care and His desire to save and preserve life, even against the backdrop of impending judgment.

The instructions on how to build the ark continue in Genesis 6.15–16, where God provides Noah with the exact dimensions and specifications for the ark's construction. This level of detail highlights God's meticulous planning and foreknowledge, ensuring that the ark would be sufficient to withstand the flood and protect its inhabitants. In Genesis 6.17, God reiterates the warning of the coming flood, emphasizing the certainty of the impending judgment.

God Initiates a Covenant

In Genesis 6.18, the tone shifts as God establishes a covenant with Noah, promising salvation for him and his family. By His willingness to initiate a covenant with Noah, God is acting as the ultimate patron – moving not for any advantage for Himself, but for the one in need. God is always acting in our interest. Here, the interest is the literal preservation of humans. Noah's responsibilities are clear, and God assures him of His presence throughout what he is about to experience. The question for Noah, *and for us today*, is how to respond.

Noah's Response

Genesis 6.22 stands as a testament to Noah's unwavering obedience. It simply says:

> And Noah did this. He did everything that God had commanded him.

We can be assured that this was not a mechanical, cold adherence to a set of divine instructions, motivated by a desire for self-preservation. Rather, it would have been a passionate, wholehearted response to God's mercy, fueled by gratitude and reverence! Noah was a man of deep faith and trust in God. He didn't just follow orders; *he surrendered control*, placing his entire trust in God's plan, even though the task at hand was unprecedented and the promise of a flood was beyond any prior human experience.

Noah's obedience was not rooted in complete understanding or clarity about the future. He had never seen an ark, nor could he fully grasp the concept of a flood capable of wiping out all of humanity and animal life. His obedience was an act of faith, *a decision to trust God implicitly*, even when the path forward was shrouded in mystery. Noah's actions demonstrate that faith is not contingent upon our understanding, but upon our trust in God's character and promises. The concept of the ark and the flood required Noah to step into the unknown, to embark on a journey of faith and obedience without a clear picture of the result. This is a powerful reminder that faith often calls us to trust God's instructions, even when we cannot see the full picture or understand the entirety of God's plan.

What the Hebrew Writer Says

Hebrews 11.7 affirms Noah's faith, describing it as alive, vibrant, and God-fearing.

> By faith Noah, being warned by God concerning events as yet unseen, in reverent fear constructed an ark for the saving of his

household. By this he condemned the world and became an heir of the righteousness that comes by faith, Hebrews 11.7.

See again how Noah is commended for his reverent response to God's warning. He is identified as an "heir of righteousness." Trust in God and obedience to His commands leads to a righteous standing before Him. Noah's faith was not passive; it was an active, living faith that propelled him to take God at His word and act accordingly.

What Drove Noah to Obey

Noah's heart was undoubtedly filled with a profound sense of gratitude, thankfulness, and love for God. These emotions were the driving force behind his obedience, motivating him to cut down the first gopher tree, to persevere through 120 years of construction amidst public scrutiny and derision, and to preach righteousness to a corrupt generation. Noah's actions were a response to God's mercy, a demonstration of his understanding that God's instructions were an extension of His grace.

In Scripture, the proclamation of the good news of what God has done *always* precedes the call to human response. In Noah's story, God's actions set the stage for Noah's obedience. God extended grace to Noah, recognizing him as being a righteous and blameless man in a corrupt generation (Genesis 6.8–9). He established a covenant with Noah, expressing His intention to save Noah and his family from the impending judgment (Genesis 6.18–21). Noah's response was one of faithful obedience, a testament to his heart that sought after God.

Noah's Legacy of Obedience

Noah's heart and his subsequent actions had far-reaching implications, not just for his immediate family, but for all of humanity. Genesis 6 serves as a foreshadowing of the salvation that would come through Jesus Christ, offering preservation from eternal death through the cross. Because Noah sought after God, chose to obey, and responded in faith, we see a powerful example of how one person's faithfulness can impact generations to come. Noah's story is a call to us, reminding us of the transformative power of faith and the enduring grace of God that calls us to respond in obedience and trust.

What's In This for Us?

Stand Firm in Faith Amidst Adversity

Noah's story teaches us the importance of maintaining our faith even when surrounded by corruption or unbelief. We must trust in God and remain steadfast in our convictions, regardless of societal pressures. Imagine living in the society described in Genesis 6.1–8, 13. How strong would your convictions be? What relevance does this have as we consider our own society and where it is headed?

We Must Pursue God

Just as Noah actively sought God, we should also be proactive in our relationship with Him. Regular prayer and quiet time reflecting on His word can help cultivate this relationship.

Trust in God's Plans

Often, we may not understand why certain things are happening in our lives. Just as Noah trusted in God's plan, despite not understanding the full scope of the flood, we should also trust in God's plan for our lives. Many times, God's plans for us might push us out of our comfort zones. In those times, like Noah, we need to step into the unknown with unwavering faith.

God's Commands are Rooted in Love and Grace

Every command or instruction from God is always given with our best interests in mind, stemming from His love and grace towards us.

Faith is Active, Not Passive

Noah's actions demonstrate that faith is about actively responding to God's commands. We too should be proactive in our relationship with God, making efforts to grow spiritually and serve others. There is always a bigger picture – one that we may not fully understand. Noah's obedience had implications far beyond his immediate situation. Similarly, our actions and faith can impact others in ways we might not immediately recognize. Always be mindful of the ripple effect your actions might have in God's bigger plan.

See the Value of Persistence

Building the ark took Noah decades. This teaches us the importance of persistence and patience, especially when working on tasks that honor God.

For Class Interaction and Discussion

Lesson Outline

1. **Introduction to Noah's story:**

    —Faith, Obedience, and Divine Grace

2. **Understanding God's Grace:**

    —Even amid judgment

3. **Communication with Noah:**

    —How God's warnings and instructions shaped the narrative

4. **God's Covenant:**

    —A binding promise of salvation

5. **Noah's Response:**

    —Act of unwavering faith

6. **Noah's Legacy:**

    —The importance of faith in our personal journey with God

Thought Questions for Discussion

1. **On Faith & Obedience:**

    a. How do you think Noah felt when he was tasked with building the ark amidst a disbelieving generation?

    b. How might you have responded if you were in Noah's shoes?

    c. Why is it important to obey God's commands even when they seem daunting or unclear?

2. **On God's Grace:**

    a. How does the story of Noah reflect the nature of God's grace?

    b. What does it mean to find favor in the eyes of the Lord?

3. **Understanding God's Commands:**

    a. What are some examples of God's commands being given in the context of grace in other biblical stories?

    b. How can we ensure we're actively seeking God's grace in our daily lives?

4. **Noah's Character:**

    a. How did Noah's character differentiate him from others during his time?

    b. In what ways can we embody the attributes of Noah in today's world?

5. **Noah's Relationship with God:**

    a. How did God's clear and detailed instructions shape Noah's faith?

    b. How do you think Noah felt knowing he had a responsibility to preserve life on Earth?

6. **Hebrews 11.7 Reflection:**

    a. How does this verse emphasize the importance of faith in the unseen?

    b. How can we develop a "reverent fear" like Noah in our relationship with God?

Group Activity:

Divide up into groups and discuss:

1. Share a time when you acted in faith, even without seeing the full picture.
2. What are some challenges we face today that require unwavering faith and trust in God?
3. How can we apply the lessons from Noah's story to our modern life?

Scripture Dive: Examine the provided passages: Hebrews 11.7; Genesis 6–7. Discuss what you see about Noah's abiding trust and dependence on God (faith) and how this applies to our lives.

Walking with God Today

This week, try to identify and reflect on one act or decision you can make based on faith, even if the outcome is uncertain.

Lesson 4

A Friend with God: Abraham

True Faith and Devotion to God

Read

Hebrews 11.8–18

Genesis 11.27—12.8

Acts 7.1–8

Overview

We are first introduced to Abram in Genesis 11. While living in Ur of the Chaldeans, God called him to leave and go to a land that He would show him, Acts 7.2–4. Abram's father Terah, his nephew Lot, and all their families started toward Canaan. For some reason they stopped in Haran and dwelt there for a few years (where Terah eventually died), before moving on to the promised land where they dwelt in tents and lived off the land.

Beginning in Genesis 12, God's plan of redemption begins to unfold. For almost 75 years, Abram played a starring role. His life became a pattern for all who came to God in faith. His was a life lived completely by faith. He is mentioned multiple times in the New Testament as a model of devotion to God. For example, Stephen started his sermon mentioning Abraham in Acts 7.1–6. Paul talked about him multiple times throughout his ministry, most notably in Romans and Galatians. The Hebrews writer also had much to say about Abraham as a hero of faith in 11.8–19.

What can we learn about Abraham? How can his life serve as an example for our own journey with God? In this lesson, we will examine four ways that illustrate the completeness of his faith.

Abraham's Pilgrimage of Faith

> By faith Abraham, when he was called, obeyed and set out for a place that he was going to receive as an inheritance. He went out, even though he did not know where he was going, Hebrews 11.8.

Faith Involves a Separation

Please see Abraham's immediate response. It is as if while the call was still coming down Abraham was already in motion. He went out not knowing where he was going. He was told he would receive an inheritance, but not where it was or what it was. Imagine the strength required. Imagine leaving everything that is familiar and everyone you know. Abraham left behind the land of his birth, his home, his estate. He severed family ties. He abandoned comfortable things. He embraced uncertainty. At this point, Abraham had no other thought on his mind but obedience. His response to God was not because someone had tried to "sell" him on Canaan once before. It was not that he knew he was going to a better place to raise his livestock or to inherit some large estate. In fact, Stephen says he never owned anything when he got there.

> He didn't give him an inheritance in it—not even a foot of ground—but he promised to give it to him as a possession, and to his descendants after him, even though he was childless, Acts 7.5.

Why did God tell Abraham to leave Ur? More importantly, out of the millions of people to choose from, why did God pick Abraham? Was there something uniquely special about him? Not really. All indications are that he would not have been too different from his father, who served multiple gods, Joshua 24.2. But when *the* Almighty God appeared to Abraham, there was no hesitation.

> Leave your country and relatives, and come to the land that I will show you. "Then he left the land of the Chaldeans and settled in Haran, Acts 7.3–4a.

Abraham immediately followed through. He believed God and a separation took place. He left. He separated himself from every bad influence and submitted to the wishes of God.

Is it Different for Us?

Jesus said:

> If anyone wants to follow after me, let him deny himself, take up his cross, and follow me, Mark 8.34.

A life of faith demands a break with everything that is familiar, everything that is old. With the help of the Spirit, we put off the old man of sin, Ephesians 4.22, and put on the qualities of Jesus in our life, Galatians 5.22–

23; Colossians 3.8–14. Our faith must begin with a willingness to separate from the world. Paul described it to the Thessalonians when he remarked how they had *turned to God from idols to serve the living and true God and to wait for his Son from heaven, whom he raised from the dead—Jesus, who rescues us from the coming wrath,* 1 Thessalonians 1.9–10. That's what we do. We turn from the world (idols) to wait. We have yet to receive our inheritance. We've been told what it is, and we've acted in faith accordingly.

We Have to Let Go of the World

The world must no longer have its grip on us. Like Paul, we must completely lose interest in it. Its cares, values, and concerns must now become secondary.

> The world has been crucified to me through the cross, and I to the world, Galatians 6.14b.

See also 1 Peter 1.13–16 and Colossians 3.1–2.

Abraham's Patient Faith

> By faith he stayed as a foreigner in the land of promise, living in tents as did Isaac and Jacob, coheirs of the same promise. For he was looking forward to the city that has foundations, whose architect and builder is God, Hebrews 11.9–10.

Abraham dwelt in Canaan as a foreigner. He did not own any land. He was nothing more than a nomad living in a tent. The land was promised to him, but he never really dwelt in it as his own possession. Yet, he never abandoned his faith in the future promise.

This is the patience of faith. The endurance to dwell in the "in-between" times. This was the challenge for him, and it is also a challenge for us. We too must remain patient. We must keep our faith strong, joyful, and full of anticipation in the time between our salvation and the ultimate moment of our glorification. Abraham never gave up in his hope. It is what drove him. It is what motivated him. Each day he pressed forward through its strength.

From Which Perspective Do You View Life?

Living with patience requires the reorientation of our focus. Are you committed to living from an eternal perspective? How do you view your trials? The first century Christians serve as a wonderful example.

> Therefore, we ourselves boast about you among God's churches—about your perseverance and faith in all the persecutions and afflictions that you are enduring, 2 Thessalonians 1.4.

James also said,

> Consider it a great joy, my brothers and sisters, whenever you experience various trials, because you know that the testing of your faith produces endurance. And let endurance have its full effect, so that you may be mature and complete, lacking nothing, James 1.2–4.

Abraham Did What We Have to Do

What keeps you going? The same thing that kept Abraham going.

> For he was looking forward to the city that has foundations, whose architect and builder is God, Hebrews 11.10.

Abraham looked for a city which was being built by God. So, since he knew he was going there, he could be patient in the land of Canaan. He could be a nomad in a foreign land. He could be a wanderer because his sights were set on the heavenly city. Therefore, Abraham did what we have to do.

> Set your minds on things above, not on earthly things, Colossians 3.2.

He was patient during his time in Canaan. There were many struggles, but he endured because his mind was not fixed with the satisfaction found in this life, he was looking for something far beyond. So must we.

Abraham Experienced the Power of Faith

> By faith even Sarah herself, when she was unable to have children, received power to conceive offspring, even though she was past the age, since she considered that the one who had promised was faithful. Therefore, from one man—in fact, from one as good as dead—came offspring as numerous as the stars of the sky and as innumerable as the grains of sand along the seashore, Hebrews 11.11–12.

From the beginning of God's dialogue with Abraham, He promised to make his descendants a great nation, Genesis 12.1–4. Not only was Abraham waiting on a place, but he was also waiting on a people. But there was a major problem. Both he and his wife were long past the age of childbearing. In this part of the story, we see the power of faith. This is a faith that sees the invisible and the impossible. It trusts in God to do what humanly cannot be done. Abraham trusted that God would be able to make this promise come true.

Faith Trusts God

We must look to Abraham as an example to follow in experiencing the power of faith. God makes promises that cannot be fulfilled on a human level and then fulfills them to those who believe in Him. This is not about looking for a miracle. It is about understanding that through His power, God can not only forgive you of your sin and make you righteous, but He can take your broken life and make you useful for His purposes. By His Spirit, He releases the power to do what seems impossible:

> Now to him who is able to do above and beyond all that we ask or think according to the power that works in us—to him be glory in the church and in Christ Jesus to all generations, forever and ever. Amen. Ephesians 3.20–21.

Abraham's Proof of Faith

> By faith Abraham, when he was tested, offered up Isaac. He received the promises and yet he was offering his one and only son, the one to whom it had been said, Your offspring will be traced through Isaac, Hebrews 11.17–18.

Imagine the strength it took to get through this test. In fact, this may be the ultimate. There is little doubt that Abraham had killed many animals for the Lord on many different occasions. But, to offer his son? In Genesis 22, we read that Abraham responded just as he always had: with immediate obedience.

It was a three-day journey for Abraham and Isaac to go to the place of sacrifice. When they finally got there, *Abraham said to his young men, "Stay here with the donkey. The boy and I will go over there to worship; then we'll come back to you,"* Genesis 22.5. See his confidence in God. The rest of the story in Genesis 22 is amazing! He knew God would raise Isaac from the dead if things had to go that far. Of this, the Hebrew writer remarks:

> He considered God to be able even to raise someone from the dead; therefore, he received him back, figuratively speaking, Hebrews 11.19.

This is an example of monumental faith. Especially considering how everything hinged on Isaac. All the promises were in him. You may ask, "Did Abraham not love Isaac?" He absolutely did, but he believed God would raise him from the dead.

What's In This for Us?

Obedience and Complete Trust

Abraham's unwavering obedience to God's commands, even when the end goal was not clear, serves as a testament to the strength of his faith. This teaches us the importance of trusting God's plan, even when it seems uncertain or daunting.

The Need for Separation

Abraham's willingness to leave behind everything familiar and head for an unknown land signifies the need for us to separate ourselves from worldly attachments and distractions. This serves as a reminder that sometimes, to truly follow God's path, we might need to step out of our comfort zones.

Patience in Waiting

Abraham's time in Canaan, living as a foreigner and nomad, illustrates the virtue of patience. Even when the promise was not immediately fulfilled, Abraham kept his faith. This highlights the importance of patience in our walk with God, trusting that His promises will be fulfilled in His time.

Living with an Eternal Perspective

Abraham's focus was not on the immediate but on the eternal city built by God. This underscores the importance of having an eternal perspective in our lives, prioritizing spiritual goals over immediate worldly gains.

Belief in the Impossible

Sarah's conception despite her age, and the subsequent birth of Isaac, demonstrates the power of faith and God's ability to accomplish His purposes. This reminds us that with God, all things are possible, and our faith can overcome seemingly insurmountable challenges.

How Far Will We Go?

Abraham's willingness to sacrifice his only son, Isaac, as a test of his faith, underscores the depth of his devotion to God. It teaches us about the sacrifices we might need to make in our spiritual life and the importance of placing God above all else.

Conclusion

What is the proof of faith? It is that which is manifested in our obedience that requires the ultimate sacrifice.

> Don't fear those who kill the body but are not able to kill the soul; rather, fear him who is able to destroy both soul and body in hell, Matthew 10.28.

How strong is your faith?

For Class Interaction and Discussion

Lesson Outline

1. **Introduction:**
   —Abraham's early life and call from God
   —New Testament references to Abraham as a model of faith
2. **Abraham's Pilgrimage of Faith:**
   —Immediate response to God's call
   —Sacrifices and the courage to move into the unknown
3. **Faith Involves a Separation:**
   —Importance of Abraham's separation from his past
   —Personal implications for believers
4. **Abraham's Patient Faith:**
   —Living in patience and anticipation of God's promises
   —Applying patience in our own spiritual journeys
5. **Abraham Experienced the Power of Faith:**
   —Sarah's miraculous childbirth
   —Trusting in God's seemingly impossible promises
6. **Abraham's Proof of Faith:**
   —The ultimate test: Sacrifice of Isaac
   —The power of unwavering trust in God's plan

Thought Questions for Discussion

1. **Introduction:**

   a. Why is Abraham frequently mentioned in the New Testament?

   b. How does Stephen reference Abraham in his sermon in Acts 7.1–6?

2. **Abraham's Pilgrimage of Faith:**

    a. What challenges might Abraham have faced when leaving everything familiar behind?

    b. Why is it significant that Abraham moved without knowing his destination?

3. **Faith Involves a Separation:**

    a. How might you relate to Abraham's experience of leaving behind the familiar?

    b. How can you practice separating from negative influences in today's world?

4. **Abraham's Patient Faith:**

    a. How can you cultivate patience in your own spiritual journey?

    b. What lessons can we learn from Abraham's time living as a nomad in Canaan?

5. **Abraham Experienced the Power of Faith:**

    a. How did Abraham and Sarah react to the seemingly impossible promise of a child?

    b. How can you trust in God's power in situations that seem beyond hope?

6. **Abraham's Proof of Faith:**
    a. How did Abraham demonstrate his unwavering faith when asked to sacrifice Isaac?

    b. How can you show your faith in challenging times?

Group Activity

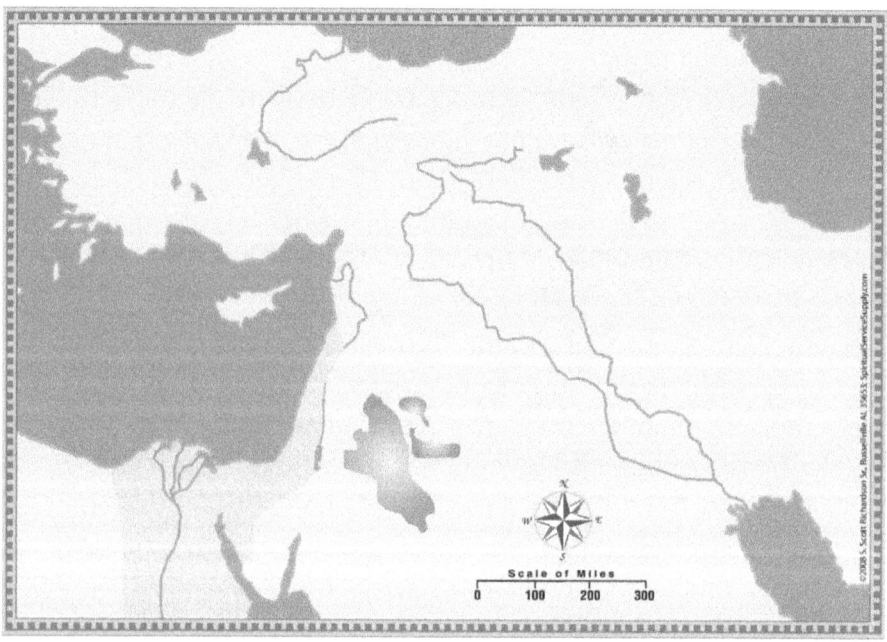

Journey Map: Sketch out Abraham's journey from Ur to Canaan. Discuss the significance of each stop along the way.

Group Discussion: Divide into groups and discuss a time when you've had to demonstrate patience or trust in God's plan, like Abraham.

Walking with God Today

Reflect on Abraham's journey and the ways his faith was tested and proven. How can his story inspire and guide your own walk with God?

Lesson 5

Trusting God's Promises: The Faith of the Patriarchs

The Legacy of Unwavering Faith

Read

Hebrews 11.20–22

Introduction

> By faith Isaac blessed Jacob and Esau concerning things to come. By faith Jacob, when he was dying, blessed each of the sons of Joseph, and he worshiped, leaning on the top of his staff. By faith Joseph, as he was nearing the end of his life, mentioned the exodus of the Israelites and gave instructions concerning his bones, Hebrews 11.20–22.

What are the *things to come* mentioned by the Hebrew writer? This certainly ties back to the promises made to Abraham in Genesis 12.1–3. There God told him that He would:

1. Give him a land to possess, 12.3.
2. Make him a great nation, 12.4.
3. Through his descendants, bless all the families of the earth, 12.5.

Genesis 25.7 records the death of Abraham at 175 years. He was buried by his sons in the cave of Machpelah, on land he had bought from the Hethites. Abraham had a full life, but never saw any of these promises come to pass. Now, the promises were handed down to his descendants. Of that, the Hebrew writer includes Isaac, Jacob, and Joseph in his great hall of fame of faith. Each of these men, like Abraham, *died in faith, although they had not received the things that were promised. But they saw them from a distance, greeted them, and confessed that they were foreigners and temporary residents on the earth,* Hebrews 11.13. They were so confident in their faith that they passed these promises on. They did not die in despair over unfulfilled dreams. They trusted that the promises would come—because they believed in God.

Hebrews 11 clearly establishes the fact that the principle of faith is not unique to the New Testament era. Faith has always been how God wants mankind to approach Him. Works have never been the way to God. We can't expect to get to heaven except through an active and living faith. *My righteous one shall live by faith*, Hebrews 10.38.

Isaac

> By faith Isaac blessed Jacob and Esau concerning things to come, Hebrews 11.20.

It is interesting to note that Isaac lived longer than any of the four patriarchs. But comparatively speaking there is little written about him. Most of his story is contained in Genesis 26–27. When placed beside his father, Isaac's life could be described as ordinary and not spectacular. His faith does not seem to be near as strong as his fathers and it appears he possessed a very passive personality.

A Life of Mistakes

Genesis 26.6–16 records Isaac's interaction with Abimelech. His fear for his own life prompted him to lie about the identity of Rebekah, so he told the men of Gerar that she was his sister. He was confronted by Abimelech when the king observed him showing affection to his wife. The king issued an edict warning the people not to harm Isaac or his wife, 26.11. As we finish up Genesis 26, through a series of moves, Isaac winds back up in the far southern reaches of the promised land: Beersheba. In Genesis 27, we have the story of Isaac and the birthright situation between Jacob and Esau.

God Blesses Isaac Despite His Imperfect Faith

Going back to Genesis 26, we observe God's continual blessing upon Isaac and his family, v. 12b–13. This was not based on Isaac's performance as much as it was based on God's promises to Abraham in Genesis 12. This is not to say Isaac was totally void of trusting God.

How Isaac Demonstrated Faith

When a famine came, Isaac heeded God's command not to go to Egypt and instead heeded God's call to *live in the land I tell you about*, 26.2. What follows in the next four verses is God's covenant with Isaac. Verse 6 details Isaac's faith matter-of-factly: *So Isaac settled in Gerar*.

Later in Genesis 26 Isaac demonstrated faith by embracing peace over conflict. Much of the second half of the chapter details a series of moves because of quarrels over water rights. Rather than seek justice or take matters into his own hands, Isaac would move on and dig another well. He demonstrated faith in God by avoiding unnecessary conflicts ... trusting that God would meet his needs.

His trust was enhanced by God's continual reassuring. After moving to Beersheba, God appeared to Isaac and said:

> I am the God of your father Abraham. Do not be afraid, for I am with you. I will bless you and multiply your offspring because of my servant Abraham, Genesis 26.24.

Like his father, Isaac responds immediately in reverence, worship, and faithful obedience:

> So he built an altar there, called on the name of the Lord, and pitched his tent there. Isaac's servants also dug a well there, Genesis 26.25.

This is why Isaac is mentioned in Hebrews 11 as an example of faith. His faith produced the knowledge to understand that the promises of God would take place. Notice his blessing of Jacob in Genesis 28.3–4:

> May God Almighty bless you and make you fruitful and multiply you so that you become an assembly of peoples. May God give you and your offspring the blessing of Abraham so that you may possess the land where you live as a foreigner, the land God gave to Abraham."

This is what the writer of Hebrews is thinking of in chapter 11, verse 20. Isaac trusted God.

Jacob

> By faith Jacob, when he was dying, blessed each of the sons of Joseph, and he worshiped, leaning on the top of his staff, Hebrews 11.21.

In essence, Jacob's life of faith could be characterized by ups and downs. Like all men, his was an imperfect faith. Sometimes he was holy. At other times his faith greatly struggled. His story is found in Genesis 28–36. What stands out about this man? His was a journey from deception to redemption. His name "Jacob" is translated *deceiver* or *supplanter*. This was especially demonstrated in his actions with his brother and father over receiving the birthright that was to be passed down from their father, Genesis 27. This action leads Jacob on a journey he never would have imagined. To avoid his brother's wrath, he had to escape, eventually winding up *in an eastern country,* 29.1, to the house of Laban, where he agreed to work for seven years in exchange for taking Laban's daughter Rachel as a wife. In his experience with Laban, the *deceiver* had to learn the hard lessons of being *deceived* by someone else. Through all of this, God was working – shaping his faith and patiently working with Jacob in the process of transformation. Jacob had to learn to trust in God's providence.

And like his father before him, Jacob pressed on … imperfectly at best … but throughout his life he responded to God's encouragement in faith. Going back to Genesis 28, when Jacob was fleeing from Esau and headed to Haran, he had a dream at Bethel where God confirmed the Abrahamic covenant with him. Jacob responded by setting up a stone pillar and vowed that if God protected and provided for him, he would give a tenth of everything he had to God. Probably one of the most significant events in Jacob's spiritual life was when he wrestled with an angel (or God Himself) at Peniel in Genesis 32. This event marked a turning point in Jacob's life. He received a new name, "Israel," and it showcased his perseverance and determination to receive a blessing from God. And finally, after many years, Genesis 35 shows how God instructed Jacob to return to his homeland. Despite fears of facing Esau and the potential consequences of past deceptions, Jacob obeyed. This action demonstrated faith in God's promise of protection and the land covenant.

While Jacob had moments of weakness and made mistakes, his life overall shows a trajectory of growth in faith and trust in God's promises. He had a genuine relationship with God that was filled with personal encounters, struggles, and ultimately, transformation.

Finally, going back to Hebrews 11.21, the blessing which passed from father to son was of great significance to the Hebrew mind. Here, the author of Hebrews sees the act as an act of faith. In the case of *Jacob*, the farewell blessings on *each of the sons of Joseph* are mentioned as particular evidence of his faith. Jacob trusted God.

Joseph

> By faith Joseph, as he was nearing the end of his life, mentioned the exodus of the Israelites and gave instructions concerning his bones, Hebrews 11.22.

Joseph's instructions concerning this are found in Genesis 50. He told the people to *pack up his bones* and take them to the Promised Land. This is some 200 years since the promises were made to Abraham. That's faith! Joseph's faith was distinct, as he believed that his descendants would eventually depart Egypt for the promised land and gave burial instructions accordingly. He held dear the promise given to Abraham, Isaac, and Jacob and expressed his own trust in it:

> Joseph said to his brothers, "I am about to die, but God will certainly come to your aid and bring you up from this land to the land he swore to give to Abraham, Isaac, and Jacob." So Joseph made the sons of Israel take an oath: "When God comes to your aid, you are to carry my bones up from here," Genesis 50.24–25.

Such a display of faith was significant and ultimately vindicated. Joseph died in Egypt, but he died in faith. The wishes of Joseph were carried out. When the exodus began, Moses gathered his bones and brought them with him on the way to Canaan. Joseph trusted God.

What's In This for Us?

Isaac, Jacob, and Joseph died victoriously

They believed God in the face of death. Death is the ultimate test. *If our faith doesn't do us any good at death, what good is it?* Basically, there are two reasons why people fear death. One is that they fear death for themselves. People fear what will happen to them after death. For the Christian, this should be no problem, for after death they go to be with the Lord, Philippians 1.21–23. People also fear death for those they will leave behind. We need to have the faith that in these situations, God will provide care and attention to those we love most. The world will move on without us. This was the approach God used with Joshua. *Moses my servant is dead. Now therefore arise, go over this Jordan, you and all this people,* Joshua 1.2. It has been said that there are presently almost 8 billion people on earth. 100 years from now they will all be dead. If Jesus doesn't return before we die, God will still be working. Everybody dies, but God lives, Jesus lives, and the work of the Spirit goes on. There is no reason to fear death because of those who are left behind. God will take care of them until it is their time to die—that is living by faith. The only reason to fear death is if you are not inside a relationship with God.

We too can die in faith

God keeps His promises. Those who live for Him can live with confidence—even if death snuffs out our physical life before Jesus returns.

We can be people of faith, even with shortcomings and mistakes

Reading Genesis 26–50 should give us hope in that the patriarchs mentioned here made many mistakes, yet God saw them as men of faith. Were they sinful? Absolutely. Duplicitous, deceitful? Certainly. Weak, vacillating, sometimes immoral? Without a doubt. But what may be true about that part of their lives doesn't cancel out what's true about the commitment they made to trust God. They could not be deterred from giving the blessing to whom the blessing belonged. Abraham would not give it to Ishmael, it went to Isaac. Isaac would not give it to Esau, it went to Jacob. Jacob would not give it to Manasseh, it went to Ephraim. They all died never having seen it. They died as strangers, wanderers, nomads, a couple of them in foreign lands.

That was the evidence of their faith. They believed God for what they couldn't see, all the way to death. This is how you believe, too, because the heaven that holds you to Christ is a heaven you have never seen. That's what it means to live by faith.

God does not save us on our perfection, but because of our relationship of faith.

Conclusion

Faith is not just about believing in the unseen, but also about trusting in the promises of God, even when they seem delayed or distant. As we reflect on the lives of the patriarchs, let us also examine our life with God and recommit to trusting God's promises.

For Class Interaction and Discussion

Lesson Outline

1. **Introduction:**

    —Understanding Faith and Its Importance in Hebrews

2. **Faith of Isaac:**

    —Trusting God Amidst Mistakes

3. **Faith of Jacob:**

    —A Journey from Deception to Redemption

4. **Faith of Joseph:**

    —Anticipating God's Promises

Thought Questions for Discussion

1. **Introduction:**

    a. How do you define faith?

    b. Why is it significant that the writer of Hebrews emphasizes faith throughout history, not just in the New Testament era?

2. **Isaac:**

    a. How does Isaac's life compare to that of his father Abraham?

    b. In what ways did Isaac demonstrate faith, and in what situations did he falter?

    c. Why do you think God continued to bless Isaac despite his imperfections?

3. **Jacob:**
    a. How does Jacob's life journey illustrate the transformative power of faith?

    b. Discuss the significance of Jacob wrestling with the angel. How can this event relate to our own spiritual struggles?

    c. How did Jacob demonstrate trust in God's promises throughout his life?

4. **Joseph:**
    a. How does Joseph's faith compare to that of his predecessors?

    b. Why is Joseph's instruction about his bones so significant in understanding his faith?

    c. How can we emulate Joseph's unwavering trust in God's promises?

5. **Thinking Things Through:**
    a. Can you think of a time in your life when you felt like the promises of God were delayed or unfulfilled?

    b. How do the stories of Isaac, Jacob, and Joseph inspire you to hold onto your faith, even during challenging times?

    c. What lessons can we draw from the mistakes and imperfections of these patriarchs?

d. How does the idea that "faith has always been how God wants mankind to approach Him" resonate with you?

e. How can we ensure that our faith is active and living, as emphasized in Hebrews 10.38?

Group Activity

Pair up with another class member and discuss the following:
   a. Share a personal experience where your faith was tested.
   b. How did you handle the situation?
   c. What lessons did you learn about trusting God's promises?

Walking with God Today

What practical steps can you take to strengthen your faith and trust in God's promises?

Lesson 6

Looking to the Reward: Moses

Making the Faithful Choice

Read

Hebrews 11.23–29

Exodus 1–2

Introduction

By faith Moses, after he was born, was hidden by his parents for three months, because they saw that the child was beautiful, and they didn't fear the king's edict. By faith Moses, when he had grown up, refused to be called the son of Pharaoh's daughter and chose to suffer with the people of God rather than to enjoy the fleeting pleasure of sin. For he considered reproach for the sake of Christ to be greater wealth than the treasures of Egypt, since he was looking ahead to the reward. By faith he left Egypt behind, not being afraid of the king's anger, for Moses persevered as one who sees him who is invisible. By faith he instituted the Passover and the sprinkling of the blood, so that the destroyer of the firstborn might not touch the Israelites. By faith they crossed the Red Sea as though they were on dry land. When the Egyptians attempted to do this, they were drowned, Hebrews 11.23–29.

Life is a series of choices that we make. Every day we are challenged to make decisions that either bring us closer to God or lead us away from Him. Which will we choose? These can be very tough decisions. John called disciples to remove their allegiance from this world. *For all that is in the world—the desires of the flesh and the desires of the eyes and pride of life—is not from the Father but is from the world. And the world is passing away along with its desires, but whoever does the will of God abides forever,* 1 John 2.16–17. There are things that faith accepts and there are things that faith rejects. Genuine, saving faith is selective. Sin is *always* a bad choice.

In today's lesson, we will examine Hebrews 11.23–29 and see the positive decisions that Moses made.

Moses Rejected the World's Prestige

While our primary focus will be from the Hebrews account, it is important to examine some key points in the historical narrative concerning Moses' birth and childhood. Exodus 1 informs us of the Egyptian Pharaoh's efforts to curtail the growing numbers of Hebrew people in his country. He instructed that all male children born in Hebrew families be killed just after they were born, Exodus 1.15–16. Two midwives, Shiphrah and Puah, refused to obey the edict. Despite the government's best efforts, God blessed the Hebrews:

> the people multiplied and grew very strong, Exodus 1.20.

To this Pharoah commanded that

> every son that is born to the Hebrews you shall cast into the Nile, but you shall let every daughter live, Exodus 1.22.

When Moses was born, his mother hid him for the first three months. After she could hide him no longer, she placed Moses inside a basket and placed it in the reeds by the riverbank. The daughter of Pharaoh came to the river to bathe and found the baby. Moses' sister, who had been dispatched to watch over him approached and asked if she should find a person to nurse the baby. She quickly found her mother. Pharaoh's daughter told her, ...*take this child and nurse him for me, and I will pay your wages. So the woman took the boy and nursed him. When the child grew older, she brought him to Pharaoh's daughter, and he became her son. She named him Moses, "Because," she said, "I drew him out of the water,"* Exodus 2.9–10a.

How long did Moses' mother have him, before she gave him back to Pharaoh's daughter? While we cannot be certain, it must have been a long period of time—some writers go as far as to speculate that Moses could have been 10–12 years old, given the language in the beginning of 2.10. What would Moses' mother have done during this time? She would have used every minute of her time to teach her son about the way of God and educate Moses about the promises to Abraham, Isaac, Jacob, and Joseph. I believe it would be very safe to say that during this time, Moses' family gave him the spiritual foundation he would have needed for the rest of his life. Once the child *grew up*, she brought the child to Pharaoh's mother who named him Moses.

The span of time between verses 10–11 may be as long as 30–35 years. Dwelling in the house of Pharaoh, the young Moses would have learned much about the worldly wisdom of Egypt. *Moses was educated in all the wisdom of the Egyptians and was powerful in his speech and actions,* Acts 7.22. He would have become fully absorbed in Egyptian culture. He had all the access and connections of royal power. Anything he wanted could have been his. But it is at this time that Moses was forced to make a tough decision.

> Years later, after Moses had grown up, he went out to his own people and observed their forced labor. He saw an Egyptian striking a Hebrew, one of his people. Looking all around and seeing no one, he struck the Egyptian dead and hid him in the sand. The next day he went out and saw two Hebrews fighting. He asked the one in the wrong, "Why are you attacking your neighbor?" "Who made you a commander and judge over us?" the man replied. "Are you planning to kill me as you killed the Egyptian?" Then Moses became afraid and thought, "What I did is certainly known," Exodus 2.11–14.

These events certainly played a role in what he determined to do. The Hebrew writer incorporates a spiritual component into Moses' decision.

> By faith Moses, when he had grown up, refused to be called the son of Pharaoh's daughter and chose to suffer with the people of God rather than to enjoy the fleeting pleasure of sin, Hebrews 11.24–25.

Moses had to choose. What would he let take hold of his heart?

The wisdom of Egypt?

The truth of God?

What he saw, or what is unseen?

We know the story. He rejected the world's prestige. It was no small decision. He was the son of Pharaoh's daughter. He dwelt inside the household of the most powerful ruler in the world. He was part of a sophisticated culture and society which was the most highly advanced of its time. He had status and wealth. Should he hold on to this? Or forsake it for what he knew was right?

Hebrews 11.24 is an act of faith. He willingly gave up the prestige, honor, power, fame, and seductive realities of this world in exchange to be identified with a group of slaves. In essence, Moses left Egypt trusting God to fulfill and accomplish His purposes in his life. That's faith. Faith rejects the world and all it has to offer. Those who serve God *no longer live for human passions, but for the will of God,* 1 Peter 4.2. Those who are not willing to let go of the world cannot come to God. The deceitfulness of riches and preoccupation of the world has led many to unfaithfulness.

Moses Rejected the World's Pleasure

Sin is enjoyable, especially if you are a prince. A person in Moses' position could have indulged in lusts at will. But Moses chose to walk away, Hebrews 11.25. We are told that he realized that the pleasures of sin are temporary: *the joy of the wicked has been brief and the happiness of the godless has lasted only a moment*, Job 20.5.

When considering our text in Hebrews 11.25, a very interesting contrast sets up when we compare Moses with David. Both men were faced with decisions. One chose to reject the passing pleasures of sin. The other did not. Think of David's choice to sin with Bathsheba. All the evidence points to a simple one-night stand. His indulgence was likely over by midnight. And yet, these few moments of pleasure had more ramifications than he could have ever imagined. At one point, in the depths of sin, David cried out, *my sin is ever before me*, Psalm 51.3. Moses made his choice by faith. What did he get? Eternal pleasures and eternal joy.

We also see that Moses rejected earthly treasures. *For he considered reproach for the sake of Christ to be greater wealth than the treasures of Egypt, since he was looking ahead to the reward*, Hebrews 11.26. This was not a rash judgment. His was a decision made from very careful consideration. Moses looked to the reward. In this, he is like Jesus in that he set it all aside to suffer ill treatment on behalf of the people of God.

Moses "Left" Egypt

The phrase in Hebrews 11.27 is significant. *By faith he **left** Egypt behind.* The **bold** word can refer to a simple departure. But there is more than that here. The wording suggests a "heart renunciation." The same word is used in Matthew 19.27. Moses was not just physically leaving Egypt; **he was renouncing Egypt.** He now rejected Egypt as having any power over his life.

Even though the king sought to kill him, Exodus 2.14, he did not leave in fear, Hebrews 11.27b. He conquered any fear he had through faith in God. In this regard, Moses stands in direct contrast to so many other Bible heroes.

- Abraham feared Abimelech and lied about his wife, Genesis 20.
- Jacob moved with fear concerning Laban, Genesis 31.
- Aaron feared the people, Exodus 32.
- David was fearful of Absalom, 2 Samuel 15.

Moses fought fear through faith in God. He trusted in what is unseen. His life is an excellent testimony to a life lived in faith. This faith caused him to make a separation. We've been called to separate from the world—which is a statement of faith. How much do we trust?

> Do not be yoked together with those who do not believe. For what partnership is there between righteousness and lawlessness? Or what fellowship does light have with darkness? What agreement does Christ have with Belial? Or what does a believer have in common with an unbeliever? And what agreement does the temple of God have with idols? For we are the temple of the living God, as God said: I will dwell and walk among them, and I will be their God, and they will be my people. Therefore, come out from among them and be separate, says the Lord; do not touch any unclean thing, and I will welcome you. And I will be a Father to you, and you will be sons and daughters to me, says the Lord Almighty, 2 Corinthians 6.14–18.

What's In This for Us?

Making Decisions by Faith

Do you make life decisions based on faith in God rather than fear of earthly consequences? What about the decisions in your career, relationships, or moral choices, where faith might lead you to make a counter-cultural or less popular choice because it aligns with your spiritual convictions?

The Value of Spiritual Foundation

Moses' upbringing by his mother, Jochebed, who instilled in him the teachings about God, demonstrates the importance of a strong spiritual foundation. How strong is your commitment of teaching your children or grandchildren about faith and the wonder of God's word?

Rejecting Temporary Pleasures for Lasting Joy

Just as Moses recognized the fleeting nature of sinful pleasure, Christians today are encouraged to seek out joy and satisfaction in that which has eternal significance. The pleasures of this life are short-term when compared with eternity. What really matters is faith and the investment of time and energy into relationships, service, and personal growth that align with the word of God. Moses chose to endure hardship with the people of God rather than enjoy the temporary pleasures of sin. When difficult circumstances come, we can face them with a hopeful perspective, looking ahead to the spiritual reward.

Overcoming Fear with Faith

Moses acted out of faith. We must not allow fear to dictate our choices, whether it be fear of others' opinions, fear of failure, or fear of loss, and instead develop a deeper trust in the guidance of God, Proverbs 3.5–8.

Conclusion

In this lesson we have been reminded of the kind of choices that define a life of faith. Moses, a man raised in the opulence of Pharaoh's palace, chose to align his heart with the people of God, rejecting the allure of sin and the treasures of Egypt. His decisions were not made lightly; they were the fruit of a faith that looked beyond the visible and temporal, to the invisible and eternal.

Moses' choices exemplify the essence of faith—a confident assurance in what we hope for and conviction about what we do not see, Hebrews 11.1. His faith was not passive; it was active and led him to actions that aligned with God's will, even when they required personal sacrifice. Moses understood that the pleasures and treasures of this world are fleeting, and he chose to invest in the eternal reward that faith in God offers.

Today, we are faced with similar choices. Will we cling to the temporary comforts and accolades that the world offers, or will we, like Moses, choose to identify with Christ, even if it means facing hardship? The faith that Moses exhibited is the same faith that we are called to live out—a faith that sees beyond the immediate, that chooses God's promises over the world's offerings, and that leads to actions that honor God.

May we, like Moses, persevere in faith, not fearing the world's reaction, but keeping our eyes fixed on the One who is invisible. And may we be encouraged by the truth that, as we make these choices of faith, we are not alone. God is with us, guiding us, and empowering us to live lives that are pleasing to Him. You can be assured of God's promise to be a Father, welcoming you as a son or daughter. Move forward in faith, trusting in God's presence and His promises, as you make choices that reflect your commitment to Him.

For Class Interaction and Discussion

Lesson Outline

1. **Introduction:**

    —Recap on the significance of Moses' life and choices

    —Connection to our daily decisions and faith

2. **Moses' Rejection of Worldly Prestige:**

    — Review of Moses' childhood (Exodus 1–2)

    — Moses' education in Egypt (Acts 7:22)

    — His ultimate decision to leave Egypt (Hebrews 11:24–25)

3. **Moses' Rejection of Worldly Pleasure:**

    — Comparison of Moses and David's choices

    — The fleeting pleasure of sin (Hebrews 11:25)

4. **Moses "Left" Egypt:**

    — The heart renunciation of Egypt (Hebrews 11:27)

    — Overcoming fear through faith

5. **Conclusion:**

    — The call to separate from the world (2 Corinthians 6:14–18)

    — Embracing a life of faith

Thought Questions for Discussion

1. What would have been some of the challenges Moses faced when growing up in Pharaoh's house?

2. How do you think Moses felt when he made the decision to leave Egypt?

3. How does Moses' decision to leave behind the wealth and status of Egypt reflect on the choices we face between worldly pleasures and spiritual integrity today?

4. Considering the faith of Moses' parents in hiding him for three months, discuss a time when you've seen faith overcome fear in your own life or in the lives of others.

5. Moses had the "education in all the wisdom of the Egyptians" but chose God's truth instead. In what ways do we encounter worldly wisdom today, and how can we discern and choose God's wisdom over it?

6. The lesson mentions that sin is a "bad choice." Discuss why the pleasures of sin are appealing and how Moses' example can help us to resist such temptations.

7. Moses is mentioned as "persevering as one who sees him who is invisible." How can we develop perseverance in our faith, especially when what we believe in is not seen?

Group Activity

1. **Group Discussion:** Think about the moment Moses decides to leave Egypt. Discuss the emotions and risks involved.
2. **Brainstorming:** Brainstorm a list of what modern equivalents of "Egypt's treasures" Christians might have to reject to follow God today.

Walking with God Today

Are there 'Egypts' that you need to leave behind? Remember, faith is about action. It's about choosing God's way, even when the world offers us its best. Choose to walk in the footsteps of Moses, with eyes fixed not on the treasures of this world, but on the eternal reward that awaits us in God's kingdom. 'For our light and momentary troubles are achieving for us an eternal glory that far outweighs them all' (2 Corinthians 4:17). Be courageous and make your decisions anchored in the faith that sees the invisible and believes the promise of God.

Lesson 7

Courageous Leadership: Joshua
A Bold, Obedient Faith

Read
Numbers 14

Joshua 3.1–17; 10.6–14; 24.14–15

Introduction

From his early days in Egypt to trials in the wilderness, and his final triumph in the Promised Land, each chapter of Joshua's life is a testament to God's wisdom and providence. The story of Joshua demonstrates the proper relationship between human obedience and divine guidance.

Joshua possessed the relentless spirit of a man chosen to stand against adversaries. His early experiences in life served as the testing ground for his faith, shaping him into Moses' trusted assistant and, ultimately, his successor. God spent decades equipping Joshua with the wisdom and fortitude needed for the greatest task of his life: leading a nation into God's promised future.

In this lesson, we will examine Joshua's early life, drawing out the enduring principles of faith, obedience, and courage that characterize his life. As we reflect on Joshua's experiences and his development under Moses' mentoring, we find guidance for our own spiritual life. We learn that leadership in God's kingdom is not born in a day but rather it is cultivated by a lifetime of faithful service and divine preparation.

Joshua's Background

Joshua was from the tribe of Ephraim and quickly rose through the ranks of the tribe's fighting men. Initially known as "Hoshea," meaning "salvation," he is given the name "Joshua" by Moses, which translates to "Yahweh saves," Numbers 13.16. It is notable that **God took 60 years to prepare Joshua for his leadership.** Joshua spent 20 years in Egypt, 40 years in the wilderness and then 50 in the Promised Land. God used the first 60 years of Joshua's life – as a slave for the Egyptians and an assistant to Moses – to prepare him to lead God's people into the Promised Land.

Exodus 17.8–13: Fighting Back the Amalekites

Already holding a leadership position within his tribe, Joshua steps into the limelight as God guides the Israelites from Egypt. During an unexpected assault by the Amalekites at Rephidim, on the way to Mt. Sinai, Joshua is tasked by Moses to muster forces and defend the people.

> At Rephidim, Amalek came and fought against Israel. Moses said to Joshua, "Select some men for us and go fight against Amalek. Tomorrow I will stand on the hilltop with God's staff in my hand," Exodus 17.8–9.

Joshua heeded Moses' command, engaging the Amalekites in battle. Meanwhile, Moses, accompanied by Aaron and Hur, ascended the hill. With Moses' hands raised, Israel prevailed. When Moses lowered his hands, Amalek prevailed. So, Moses kept his hands high. As his strength waned, a stone was provided for him to sit upon, and Aaron and Hur supported his hands, one on each side, ensuring they remained held high until dusk. Consequently, Joshua's forces triumphantly routed the Amalekite army, Exodus 17.8–13.

Exodus 33.11: Serving as Moses' Assistant

After this, Joshua becomes known as Moses' assistant, remaining at his side during significant moments like the receiving of the Ten Commandments on the mountain, Exodus 24.13, and even while Moses communicated with God in the Tent of Meeting.

> The Lord would speak with Moses face to face, just as a man speaks with his friend, then Moses would return to the camp. His assistant, the young man Joshua son of Nun, would not leave the inside of the tent, Exodus 33.11.

Later, an incident revealing Joshua's fervent spirit occurs when the Spirit of God descends upon some of the elders.

> A young man ran and reported to Moses, "Eldad and Medad are prophesying in the camp." Joshua son of Nun, assistant to Moses since his youth, responded, "Moses, my lord, stop them!" But Moses

asked him, "Are you jealous on my account? If only all the Lord's people were prophets and the Lord would place his Spirit on them," Numbers 11.27–29.

Numbers 14.8–9: One of the 12 Spies

When it was time to scout the Promised Land, Joshua represented the tribe of Ephraim, and Caleb, the tribe of Judah. Contrary to the ten scouts who discouraged the Israelites, Joshua, along with Caleb, stood firm in faith, urging the people to trust in God and seize the land, Numbers 14.8–9.

Numbers 27.18–23: Appointed as Moses' Successor

By the time we get to Numbers 27, the moment had arrived for Moses to appoint his successor.

> The Lord replied to Moses, "Take Joshua son of Nun, a man who has the Spirit in him, and lay your hands on him. Have him stand before the priest Eleazar and the whole community, and commission him in their sight. Confer some of your authority on him so that the entire Israelite community will obey him. He will stand before the priest Eleazar who will consult the Lord for him with the decision of the Urim. He and all the Israelites with him, even the entire community, will go out and come back in at his command." Moses did as the Lord commanded him. He took Joshua, had him stand before the priest Eleazar and the entire community, laid his hands on him, and commissioned him, as the Lord had spoken through Moses, Numbers 27.18–23.

Following the God's directive, Moses presented Joshua to Eleazar the priest and the congregation, laying hands on him to inaugurate his leadership, in accordance with God's command. It's noteworthy that the Spirit of the Lord was already with Joshua before his formal commissioning, Numbers 27.18, but with Moses' consecration, Joshua is fully empowered to lead the people of Israel.

Deuteronomy 31.7–8: Fully commissioned as the new leader by Moses

This important passage must not be passed over:

> Moses then summoned Joshua and said to him in the sight of all Israel, "Be strong and courageous, for you will go with this people

into the land the LORD swore to give to their ancestors. You will enable them to take possession of it. The LORD is the one who will go before you. He will be with you; he will not leave you or abandon you. Do not be afraid or discouraged," Deuteronomy 31.7–8.

Here is the official transition of leadership from Moses to Joshua. Moses publicly recognized and affirmed Joshua as the new leader. This was not just a private endorsement but a national declaration. Moses established Joshua's authority in the sight of the people, which would have been crucial for his acceptance as the leader. The authority with which Joshua led was not based on his own design but was given by God. This divine commissioning was foundational for Joshua's role and for the people's willingness to follow him. It emphasizes that Joshua was not merely Moses' replacement; he was God's chosen leader.

Joshua was commanded to be strong and courageous. The role came with immense challenges. The encouragement to be courageous implied that there would be fearsome tasks ahead and significant obstacles, but Joshua was to face them head-on. Joshua was assured of God's continuous presence. The promise that the Lord would go before him, be with him, and never forsake him was an assurance of divine guidance and provision. God's power would sustain him and help him overcome fear. It was a reassurance to Joshua that his strength and success would come from God, not from his own capabilities.

For Joshua, this moment would have been seen as a threshold, where he stepped out of Moses' shadow into his own calling. It symbolized the transfer of leadership and the assurance that the same God who guided Moses would now be with Joshua. For the people, it represented a continuity of purpose and divine presence, despite the change in human leadership.

Courage Exemplified

Joshua Trusted God

Numbers 14.6–9: The Faithful Report of the Promised Land

The book of Numbers provides us with a powerful exhibition of faithfulness and courage from Joshua and Caleb, which stood in great contrast to the fear and rebellion exhibited by the other spies and the Israelite people. Twelve spies were sent to survey the land of Canaan, which God had promised to the Israelites. While ten of the spies report back with a faithless report, highlighting the strength and size of the Canaanites and their fortified cities, Joshua and Caleb presented a report characterized by faith and courage.

Joshua defied the majority's faithlessness. Tearing his clothes, a traditional sign of mourning and distress, he publicly disagreed with the ten other spies. Joshua didn't just offer a differing opinion; he demonstrated a willingness to stand alone, rooted in faith despite the overwhelming tide of popular opinion leaning toward fear and disobedience.

See also how **Joshua affirmed God's promise**. He reminded the people of the goodness of the land that had been surveyed. The description "exceedingly good" is not just about the fertility or beauty of the land but also an affirmation of God's promise. Joshua saw the land through the lens of God's faithfulness, not through the intimidating presence of its current inhabitants.

Next, think of how **Joshua and Caleb's courage is directly connected to their trust in God's attitude toward Israel**. They believed that if God was pleased with them, He would not only bring them into the land but ensure their conquest and settlement. The core of their courage was the conviction that God was with them. While the other spies saw the military might and the fortifications of the inhabitants, Joshua and Caleb saw that such human strength was nothing compared to the presence of God.

Finally consider how **they implored the people not to rebel against God**, equating succumbing to fear and refusing to enter the land as spiritual rebellion. The actions of the people and the faithless spies revealed how they had turned against God's plan and God's promises.

A Man of Faith

Joshua 3.7–17: The Jordan River Crossing

The Jordan River crossing became a defining moment for Joshua at the very beginning of his role as the leader of Israel. Here the people stood at the threshold of the Promised Land, facing the Jordan River at flood stage. This event mirrored the Red Sea crossing under Moses and signifying a new chapter under Joshua's guidance.

> The Lord spoke to Joshua: "Today I will begin to exalt you in the sight of all Israel, so they will know that I will be with you just as I was with Moses," Joshua 3.7.

What would happen on this day would be a clear signal to the people that the same miraculous power that led them out of Egypt was still at work. The act of crossing the Jordan was both a literal and symbolic entry into a new land and a new era. Joshua's courage is not only seen in facing the fearful obstacle of the river but also in the moment of transition and the expectation of fulfilling Moses' legacy. To step into the shoes of Moses and to undertake a similar miracle of parting waters, required immense faith.

As Joshua communicated God's instructions and led the priests carrying the Ark of the Covenant to step into the waters of the Jordan, his courage is evident. The priests' feet touch the water's edge, and the waters from upstream stop flowing, piling up in a heap—an incredible demonstration of God's power, Joshua 3.13–16. His leadership in this act is unmistakable, displaying absolute confidence in God's promise.

The crossing of the Jordan under Joshua's command points the actualization of the promises made to Abraham, Isaac, and Jacob. Israel will now transition from wandering in the wilderness to claiming their inheritance. Joshua's courage is seen in his steadfast reliance on God's word and a deep conviction of His faithfulness to His promises.

A Man of Bold and Decisive Action
Joshua 10.6–14: Confronting the Five Amorite Kings

Joshua 10.6–14 details another moment where Joshua demonstrated remarkable courage and faith, leading the Israelites against a formidable alliance of five Amorite kings. These Canaanite leaders had mobilized to punish the Gibeonites for making peace with Israel, prompting them to appeal to Joshua for help.

Verses 6–8 showcase his boldness because of God's continual assurance:

> Then the men of Gibeon sent word to Joshua in the camp at Gilgal: "Don't give up on your servants. Come quickly and save us! Help us, for all the Amorite kings living in the hill country have joined forces against us." So Joshua and all his troops, including all his best soldiers, came from Gilgal. The Lord said to Joshua, "Do not be afraid of them, for I have handed them over to you. Not one of them will be able to stand against you."

Joshua led a surprise all-night march from Gilgal to Gibeon. Not only did he respond without delay, but he also chose to march under the cover of darkness, demonstrating his confidence in God's promise and a clear strategy to catch the Amorites unprepared.

When Joshua and his army arrived, God threw the enemy into chaos with a hailstorm that claimed more lives than the sword of the Israelites themselves, Joshua 10.11 While the battle raged, Joshua called upon the Lord to halt the sun and moon.

> On the day the Lord gave the Amorites over to the Israelites, Joshua spoke to the Lord in the presence of Israel: "Sun, stand still over Gibeon, and moon, over the Valley of Aijalon." And the sun stood still and the moon stopped until the nation took vengeance on its enemies. Isn't this written in the Book of Jashar? So the sun stopped in the middle of the sky and delayed its setting almost a full day. There has been no day like it before or since, when the Lord listened to a man, because the Lord fought for Israel. Then Joshua and all Israel with him returned to the camp at Gilgal, Joshua 10.12–15.

Joshua's leadership in this moment was so much more than military skills; it reflected a deep conviction that God's power can and will ensure the completion of the mission God gave him. He didn't waver in the face of overwhelming odds or even the natural order of creation. He knew God would act on behalf of His people. See his confidence later in the chapter when the time came to execute the five Amorite kings. He tells his army:

> When they brought the kings out to Joshua, Joshua summoned all the Israelites, and said to the chiefs of the warriors who had gone with him, "Come near, put your feet on the necks of these kings." Then they came near and put their feet on their necks. And Joshua said to them, "Do not be afraid or dismayed; be strong and courageous; for thus the Lord will do to all the enemies against whom you fight," Joshua 10.24–25.

Joshua Toward the End of His Life

This lesson would not be complete without considering Joshua's words in chapter 24:

> "Therefore, fear the Lord and worship him in sincerity and truth. Get rid of the gods your ancestors worshiped beyond the Euphrates River and in Egypt, and worship the Lord. But if it doesn't please you to worship the Lord, choose for yourselves today: Which will

you worship—the gods your ancestors worshiped beyond the Euphrates River or the gods of the Amorites in whose land you are living? As for me and my family, we will worship the Lord," Joshua 24.14–15.

Here Israel stood on the cusp of fully inhabiting the land of Canaan. Joshua has led them all the way from the wilderness wanderings to settlement. At this moment he confronted the people with a choice that is as much about loyalty as it is about faith. His faith is the culmination of a lifetime of service and dedication to the Lord. He had been a firsthand witness to the wonders, trials, and providence of God. He had seen the Red Sea part, manna descend from heaven, and the walls of Jericho fall. Each of these amazing experiences strengthened his trust in the Lord, and he stood before Israel as a testament to unwavering faith.

In calling Israel to "fear the Lord and worship him in sincerity and truth," Joshua is asking them to walk firmly in the path that he has walked before them—paved by trust, loyalty, and obedience. His challenge to put away the gods of their ancestors is a direct call to reject the visible and tangible for the invisible and intangible promises of God, a move that requires faith.

Joshua was completely committed to this faith. His faith was not passive; it was a dynamic, active force that compelled him to take a stand. This was a faith of total devotion; the kind of faith that characterized Joshua's leadership from his days as a spy in Canaan to his old age as the people's guide in the promised land.

What's In This for Us?

Seek God's Guidance

Just as Joshua sought God's direction before making decisions, we should also cultivate a habit of prayer and seeking God's wisdom in our choices, large and small.

Courage Over Comfort

Joshua's life was marked by stepping out of his comfort zone, from being a spy to leading a nation. We must develop the kind of faith that will allow us to face our fears, take on new challenges, and trust God's strength rather than our own, Ephesians 6.10.

Obedience to God's Word

Joshua was committed to following God's commands. We should similarly prioritize obedience to Scripture and let it guide our actions and decisions. Faith demonstrates its dependence on God through obedience.

Remember God's Faithfulness

Joshua set up stones as a reminder of God's faithfulness. We can keep a journal or maintain other physical reminders of the ways God has worked in our lives to encourage us in tough times.

End with God

Joshua ended his life by recommitting himself and the people to God. In our lives, we should routinely reaffirm our commitment to God, remembering that our ultimate purpose is to serve Him.

Conclusion

In conclusion, the life and leadership of Joshua are a testimony to the importance of courage, faith, and reliance on God throughout our life. His story serves as an enduring example of godly character and steadfastness in the face of adversity. As we reflect on the different chapters of Joshua's life—from his time as Moses' assistant, to his role as a spy, and eventually as the leader who led the Israelites into the Promised Land—we see a pattern of divine preparation and faith in action.

Joshua's unwavering trust in God's promises, even against incredible odds, stands as an encouragement to us today. The same God who parted the Red Sea and the Jordan River, who guided Joshua's strategies and gave him victory over the Amorite kings, is present in the lives of Christians today, calling us to be strong and courageous in our faith. Joshua's example challenges us to trust in God's timing, to seek His presence continuously, and to lead by serving others faithfully.

The legacy of Joshua's faith—a legacy of courage, obedience, and a life devoted to following God—is worth our consideration. Just as he led a whole nation to inherit the promises of God, we too are called to live lives that point others toward the faithfulness of God and the certainty of His promises.

For Class Interaction and Discussion

Lesson Outline

1. **Joshua's Background:**
   - Exodus 17.8–13—Battle Against the Amalekites
   - Exodus 33.11—Joshua's Role as Moses' Assistant
   - Numbers 14.8–9—Joshua as One of the 12 Spies
   - Numbers 27.18–23—Joshua Appointed as Moses' Successor
   - Deuteronomy 31.7–8—The Commissioning of Joshua

2. **Overview of Joshua's Display of Courage:**
   - Numbers 14.6–9—His Faithful Report
   - Joshua 3.7–17—At the Red Sea Crossing
   - Joshua 10.6–14—Boldness in the Face of Great Opposition

3. **Joshua at the End of His Life:**

Thought Questions for Discussion

1. Reflect on the significance of Joshua's original name "Hoshea" and the change to "Joshua". What does this reveal about the role of divine purpose in our identities?

2. In what ways can we emulate Joshua's dedication and service as seen during his time as Moses' assistant?

3. Contrast the response of Joshua and Caleb to the other ten spies. How does this speak to the role of faith in confronting challenges?

4. Discuss how Joshua's appointment as Moses' successor illustrates the principle of spiritual mentorship and succession planning in leadership.

5. What does "be strong and courageous" mean to you in the context of your personal life and spiritual walk?

6. How did Joshua's faith in God's promises affect his leadership decisions during key moments such as the crossing of the Jordan River?

7. Analyze the scenario of Joshua's prayer for the sun to stand still. How does this inform our understanding of prayer and God's power?

Group Activity

Group Discussion: Discuss how trust in God is like or different from the trust we place in others.

Walking with God Today

As we close today's lesson on Joshua, remember that the same God who was with Joshua is with us today. His promises are real, His presence is sure, and His power is unmatched. As Joshua did, let us serve faithfully in the roles we are given, for in due time, God prepares us for greater tasks. Stand firm in your faith, even when others may waver, and remember that your courage comes from the Lord. Be strong and courageous, not because of your strength, but because of His presence with you.

Lesson 8

Harlot to Heroine: Rahab

Great Faith Leads to Great Deliverance

Read

Hebrews 11.31

Joshua 2

Introduction

We are first introduced to Rahab in Joshua 2.1–11 as she hid the spies sent by Joshua before Israel conquered Jericho. In the New Testament, she is mentioned several times.

- Matthew includes her in the genealogy of Jesus, Matthew 1.5.
- She is mentioned in connection with heroic faith in Hebrews 11.31.
- James mentions her as having been justified through works, James 2.25.

Before her life of faith, she had some character issues to contend with as she worked as a prostitute and lied to hide the spies. What can we learn about Rahab? How did a Canaanite woman, with a terrible past, wind up in the genealogy of Christ? How did she find herself in the heroes of faith section of Hebrews 11? How can she be an inspiration to us today? What can we learn about her life?

Rahab's name means "insolence" or "fierceness." It is believed that the "ra" part of her name comes from Egyptian idolatry. "Ra" was the sun god. She lived in the walled city of Jericho, which was around five miles from the Jordan river. The city was well supplied with water and was in a fertile plain just east of a barren mountain range. Joshua 2.15 says that Rahab lived inside the wall of the city, and the record says the house had a roof area, as well as a window facing the outside. She and her entire family lived in the same dwelling place, 2.13; 6.23.

A Heart Affected by Truth

In Joshua 2.9–11 we read,

> "I know that the LORD has given you this land and that the terror of you has fallen on us, and everyone who lives in the land is panicking because of you. For we have heard how the LORD dried up the water of the Red Sea before you when you came out of Egypt, and what you did to Sihon and Og, the two Amorite kings you completely destroyed across the Jordan. When we heard this, we lost heart, and everyone's courage failed because of you, for the LORD your God is God in heaven above and on earth below.

This statement sheds light on what the Hebrew writer said in Hebrews 11.31:

> By faith Rahab the prostitute did not perish with those who were disobedient, because she had received the spies in peace, Hebrews 11.31.

Think about how our souls can be affected by the truth. Impressions made can quickly wear off. The inhabitants of Jericho were deeply stirred by reports of God's judgments on the wicked. They feared that their turn was next. Their hearts melted within them. We may wonder why they did not repent and cry out for mercy when Israel approached. For insight on this, Solomon's writing comes to mind: *Because sentence against an evil deed is not executed speedily, the human heart is fully set to do evil*, Ecclesiastes 8.11–13. Every day for six days, the people of Jericho had the opportunity to repent. As those days passed, the wall remained as strong as they always had. Maybe they felt as secure as ever.

So, what made Rahab different?

She was convinced by the evidence. She knew God was God. But not only did she know and understand the evidence, her heart was willing to submit to the evidence. Her faithful obedience saved her. The principles communicated in Romans 6.17 and Hebrews 5.8–9 ring forever true.

Rahab Moved with Conviction

In 2.17–18, Rahab hung a scarlet cord from her window until Israel returned. Everyone would have seen it. Her extended family would have had to be there when the city was conquered. What would have happened had one of them leaked information to the authorities? Add to this, what happened when Israel approached. When they got there, they simply marched around the city for six days. Rahab would not have known the plan. She would not have known that on the seventh day the walls would fall. What if she gave up?

Faith has always been an expensive commitment. Think of these Bible characters who were willing to go the distance—under trying and stressful circumstances:

- Abraham and Isaac—Genesis 22.
- Shadrach, Meshach, and Abednego—Daniel 3.
- Daniel—Daniel 6.
- Stephen—Acts 7.

Would we be faithful if it meant losing our life? Consider these passages: Matthew 16.24-26; 10.32-39. Paul said he was willing to die for his faith—Acts 21.13. Consider the test the Christians at Smyrna were asked to follow through with—Revelation 2.10. This is much more than secret belief—it is confidence in God that leads to bold action.

God Can Save the Worst of Sinners

Rahab's lifestyle before her association with the Israelites is one of those that were described as a grave sin. Harlotry was used as an example to portray the unfaithfulness of Israel and under the law it was punishable by death. But, in our story we see a wonderful example of God's grace. When Rahab moved by faith and obeyed God she was saved.

The Bible is full of stories of deliverance.

- Paul, the chief of sinners, was made free by the blood of Christ—1 Timothy 1.12-15.
- The Corinthians were guilty of several awful sins—but were washed, sanctified, and justified—1 Corinthians 6.9-11.
- Jesus made it His mission to save the lost—Luke 5.32; 19.10.

Rahab's lifestyle of sin carried as much weight as any other sin. Harlotry is no worse than stealing, murder, foul language, or idle gossip. All sin is sin and will separate us from God. The gospel has the power to save the worst of sinners. (Paul is a great example, 1 Timothy 1.15.) Often the worst of sinners make the best Christians! We cannot underestimate the power of the gospel. It has the power to fully change who we are. While some might think that a harlot, such as Rahab, would be an unlikely example of how to become a strong Christian, it's proof that God will save the worst of the worst—if they will humbly submit to Him.

What About Her Lie?

There are many explanations that run the spectrum. Some explain Rahab's actions and argue that *lying is acceptable in certain situations.* Others say, *sometimes we must choose the lesser of two evils.* Still others say *sometimes we must choose the greater of two goods.*

What are some important things to remember as we think about Rahab's actions?

First, know that scripture's approval of righteous deeds by individuals should not be taken as an endorsement of all their actions. Even notable figures like Noah, Abraham, and Moses had moments of disobedience. Every person has the potential to be faithful despite their sins and imperfections. The apostle Peter, despite his flaws, was chosen to preach the gospel.

We should also consider the depravity of Canaanite culture, of which Rahab was a part. The Canaanites engaged in abominable customs and idolatry. Rahab's profession as a harlot and her dishonesty should be placed in the context of this sinful culture.

At the time of Israel's invasion, Rahab was entering into a transition from a pagan lifestyle to embracing the one true God and His ways. She believed in the Lord's power and demonstrated courage by aiding Israelite spies and shielding them from capture. Hers, like everyone's, is an imperfect faith. Rahab's evolving faith deserves recognition and praise.

Rahab's story should not be misinterpreted as a justification to lie. Rather, we should recount her life to highlight the supremacy of Jehovah over the false gods of the world and to encourage God's followers to move in boldness, trusting the Lord.

What's In This for Us?

Seek Repentance and Transformation

Just as Rahab turned from her sinful past and embraced faith in God, we need to recognize the need for repentance and transformation in our own lives. What are some areas where you need to make changes and what steps are needed to more align your life with God's principles?

Embrace Truth and Obedience

Rahab's heart was affected by the truth when she heard about God. Today we actively seek God's truth by taking in the word help us, Colossians 3.16, and allow it to shape our beliefs and actions. Because Christ is the Lord of our life, we commit to obedience to God's commands, even when it's challenging.

Believe in the Power of God's Grace

Rahab's story illustrates God's grace to save even the worst of sinners. No one is beyond God's reach, and His grace has the power to transform lives. The gospel is a message of hope!

Commit to Continuous Growth

Rahab's faith was a process of growth and change. Recognize that faith is not static; it's a lifelong journey. Commit to continuous spiritual growth, learning, and development in your relationship with God.

Conclusion

Joshua 6.22–23 provides evidence that Rahab's faith was rewarded. She was not only preserved from destruction, but *she dwelt in Israel* after Jericho was destroyed. She went from being a citizen of heathen Jericho—to a place inside the congregation of the Lord. Later, she became the honored wife of a prince in Judah, the mother of Boaz, and one of the grandmothers of David.

From the depths of sin and shame, she was delivered because of God's grace and her own belief and repentance. She went from absolute bottom to the height of honor and dignity. Truly the rewards of faith are most excellent and glorious.

How strong is your faith? Are you willing to submit to God?

For Class Interaction and Discussion

Lesson Outline
1. **Introduction:**

2. **A Heart Affected by Truth:**

    —What made Rahab different?

    —Her faithful obedience saved her

3. **Rahab Moved with Conviction:**

    —Faith has always been an expensive commitment

    —Confidence in God leads to bold action

4. **God Can Save the Worst of Sinners:**

    —Here we see a wonderful example of grace

    —We cannot underestimate the power of the gospel

5. **What About Her Lie?**

Thought Questions for Discussion

1. What can we learn from Rahab's transformation and her inclusion in Christ's genealogy?

2. How can the truth affect our hearts and lead to genuine repentance?

3. What motivates people to resist repentance even when confronted with the truth?

4. What does Rahab's courage and commitment teach us about unwavering faith?

5. How does the power of the gospel manifest in the transformation of sinners like Rahab?

6. How should we approach ethical dilemmas like Rahab's lie considering biblical principles?

7. What lessons can we draw from Rahab's story about the rewards of faith and God's grace?

Group Activity

Reflect on the ethical dilemmas presented in the lesson and discuss how we should apply the principle that scriptural approval of righteous deeds doesn't endorse all actions. How should we proceed when we face ethical challenges?

Rahab's story is a testament to bold faith in the face of adversity. In your group, discuss ways to encourage one another to step out in faith, how to develop trust in God during challenging situations, and to be more willing to make sacrifices for the sake of your faith.

Walking with God Today

Rahab's journey from a sinful past to a place of honor and dignity within God's plan demonstrates the incredible power of faith. Her story reminds us that no one is beyond redemption, and what God promises is truly excellent and glorious. Use Rahab's courage and commitment to inspire you to submit to God's truth and embrace a life of faith.

Lesson 9

Faith to Follow Through: Gideon

From Fear to Faith

Read

Judges 6–8

Hebrews 11.32–34

Introduction

In Hebrews 11.32–34 we read:

And what more should I say? For time would fail me to tell of Gideon, Barak, Samson, Jephthah, of David and Samuel and the prophets— who through faith conquered kingdoms, administered justice, obtained promises, shut the mouths of lions, quenched raging fire, escaped the edge of the sword, won strength out of weakness, became mighty in war, put foreign armies to flight.

Five of the men listed here have their stories told in the book of Judges. In our minds, we may have a certain image we envision when we think of the word judge. The Hebrew term translated as "judge" is not just about passing judgments; it primarily signifies a "deliverer." The judges were individuals appointed by God to safeguard, shield, and rescue Israel from their adversaries. They weren't legal scholars or lawyers chosen for their legal expertise. They earned their reputation through their military achievements, powered by God, as they conquered enemies and defended Israel. We should view them as saviors, deliverers, and warriors rather than politicians or monarchs. Their role resembled that of a military general more than a political leader or ruler.

The entire era can be characterized by the closing verse of Judges, found in Judges 21.25. It reads, "In those days, there was no king in Israel," signifying the period between Moses, Joshua, Saul, and David when there was no centralized monarchy. The verse continues, "Everyone did what was right in his own eyes," portraying a chaotic time when people acted independently without a uniform governing authority. This era is also marked by the cycle of faithfulness, a drifting into unfaithfulness, oppression by an enemy, the people crying out for deliverance, and God sending a judge to rescue them out of the hands of their oppressor. This cycle repeated itself for almost 400 years.

The story of Gideon unfolds in Judges 6-8, who lived during a time when the Israelites were dealing with seven years of occupation by the Midianites. Heavily oppressed, the Israelites beseech the Lord for assistance, prompting God to remind them of His past deeds on their behalf, Judges 6.1-10. Through Gideon's story, we discover valuable lessons about obedience to God, even in moments of doubt.

God Calls Gideon into Action

Gideon's story opens in Judges 6.11. He is threshing wheat inside a winepress to hide it from the Midianites. A winepress is typically used for crushing grapes, not for threshing wheat. Threshing wheat is typically done on an open hilltop, where the wind can separate the chaff from the grain. So, why was Gideon attempting to thresh wheat in a winepress? He wanted to protect his wheat from the constant threat of the Midianites. They were a constant menace, and Gideon is so concerned about their potential raids that he chose to work in a concealed winepress rather than in the open, where he could be easily spotted, and his wheat stolen. He fears the looming presence of these enemy raiders who are always on the lookout, ready to seize his wheat, and even pose a danger to his life.

Suddenly and without warning, the angel of the Lord appears with him inside the winepress. *The Lord is with you, valiant warrior*, 6.12. Gideon probably wasn't feeling much like a warrior. In your mind can you see him looking around and saying, "Who, me?" In the next verse he does gather the courage to ask why God was allowing the Midianites to overtake Israel. To this the angel of the Lord replied:

> "Go in the strength you have and deliver Israel from the grasp of Midian. I am sending you!"

Then Gideon says,

> "Please, Lord, how can I deliver Israel? Look, my family is the weakest in Manasseh, and I am the youngest in my father's family," Judges 6.15.

At this point in his life, Gideon has no great faith, no noble warrior spirit, and no valiant courage. His is a natural human response. He was not part of an influential family. He was the youngest in the family. Surely there were many others with far superior qualifications. What could he possibly do against the powerful Midianite army? His response is much like Moses' in Exodus 3.11. He was a weak man; but the angel called him a man of valor, not for what he was, but for what he would become. God saw his potential. He looks beyond our sin and weakness and sees what He will do with our life if we yield it fully to Him. See how God graciously reassures Gideon:

> "But I will be with you," the Lord said to him. "You will strike Midian down as if it were one man," Judges 6.16.

He would overcome them all together, as one.

Gideon's Journey of Doubt and Faith

Gideon is still not convinced. He asks for a sign, 6.17. Gideon offers meat and bread to the angel of the Lord, and it was consumed with fire. Then the angel vanished, 6.19-21. This was the sign that Gideon needed and finally, *he got it*. In 6.22 He says:

> "Oh no, Lord God! I have seen the angel of the Lord face to face!"

The Lord assures him he will not die. Gideon built an altar and gave it the name Yahweh-Shalom, signifying "The Lord is peace," 6.23-24.

Over the next few verses, we learn how God prepared Gideon to be a leader through a series of tests.

Tearing down the altar of Baal

Gideon is instructed to tear down his father's altar to Baal and replace it with an altar to the Lord. He should have done it sooner. The whole reason for the Midianite oppression was their idolatry. He was fearful, but he obeyed the Lord. He and ten men snuck in and tore down the altar in the dark. Courage was not something Gideon knew well; but he did what he was told because he had met a divine visitor. The next day the men of the city wanted to kill Gideon. His father arose and defended him saying, if Baal was a god, let him defend himself because someone tore down his altar. Crisis averted.

The Wool Fleece Sign

Soon afterward the Midianites and Amalekites and other eastern warriors gathered against Israel. Gideon summoned the men of Israel to fight. 32,000 men responded. Gideon is still afraid. He placed a wool fleece on the threshing floor and said if the dew was on the fleece only and the floor was dry, he would know the Lord was with him, 6.37. God answers his request.

When he got up early in the morning he squeezed the fleece and wrung dew out of it, filling a bowl with water, 6.38. This still wasn't good enough for Gideon. He requested that the next night God do the opposite by allowing the dew to be all over the ground, but leaving the fleece dry, 6.39. *That night, God did as Gideon requested: only the fleece was dry, and dew was all over the ground,* 6.40. God's patience is an amazing thing.

This is not noble; this is doubt. Gideon's action is not what believers should do. We don't put the Lord to the test. We don't ask Him for miraculous signs to prove His Word. We trust His Word. We live by faith and obedience to His Word.

Leader of an Unconventional Army

When going to war, military strategists want to have the best forces, weapons, and plans. They want to have every advantage on their side to make victory more likely. But God doesn't work like that. In this case, having superior forces would have been a problem. He wanted all the glory to go to Him when His people won a battle. If they won because they had more soldiers or better weapons, they would be proud and say that they won by their own power. Here God is reiterating what he had told the people by Moses years before:

> "When you go out to war against your enemies and see horses, chariots, and an army larger than yours, do not be afraid of them, for the Lord your God, who brought you out of the land of Egypt, is with you," Deuteronomy 20.1.

So, the process of trimming down the battle force begins. First there was a call for those who were timid and afraid to leave, resulting in the departure of 22,000 men, 7.3. Only 10,000 men remained. Next, God says that is too many. So, Gideon is told to bring the troops down to the water where they would be tested. God says:

> "Separate everyone who laps water with his tongue like a dog. Do the same with everyone who kneels to drink." The number of those who lapped with their hands to their mouths was three hundred men, and all the rest of the troops knelt to drink water, Judges 7.5b-6.

Of the remaining 10,000 warriors, God sent 9700 of them home, leaving only the 300 who lapped water in an unconventional way. Now, imagine if you are Gideon at this moment. To reassure him, God commands him to sneak into the Midianite camp. The number of fighters was as a *swarm of locusts, and their camels were as innumerable as the sand on the seashore,* 7.12. When Gideon and his servant Purah arrived near the camp they overheard two men talking about a dream one of them had. The second man explained that the dream was about Gideon's victory that God would give him, 7.13-14. When Gideon heard this, he raced back to his camp, rallied his men, and the 300 attacked them and God gave them the victory.

What's In This for Us?

Obedience Despite Doubt

Like Gideon, we may have doubts about our abilities and God's call to faithful trust. However, God can use us when we follow through, even in uncertainty.

God's Strength in Weakness

God often chooses the humble and unlikely to accomplish His purposes. Our weaknesses can become a platform for God's strength and glory.

Giving Credit to God

Gideon's reduced army highlighted the importance of giving credit to God for our victories. Let us always acknowledge God's role in our successes. You stand in the strength of His might, Ephesians 6.10.

Overcoming Fear

Just as Gideon overcame fear, we should confront our fears with faith in God's presence and promises. Trusting in God's peace can help us face challenges boldly.

Conclusion

Gideon's journey from fear to faith reminds us that God can work through our doubts and weaknesses. When we submit to His call and trust in His strength, we can overcome obstacles and achieve victories for His glory. Like Gideon, let us recognize that God's presence and power are with us, even in our moments of uncertainty.

For Class Interaction and Discussion

Lesson Outline

1. **Understanding the Role of Judges:**

    —The Chaotic Era of Judges

2. **Gideon's Humble Beginnings:**

    —Gideon's Doubt and God's Call

    — Gideon's Tests and Obedience

3. **Leading an Unconventional Army:**

4. **Lessons for Our Lives:**

Thought Questions for Discussion

1. How does the term "judge" in the book of Judges differ from the modern understanding of a judge? What responsibilities did these judges have beyond legal matters?

2. What does it mean when the Bible says, "Everyone did what was right in his own eyes" during the time of the Judges? How can a lack of centralized authority impact a society?

3. How did Gideon's initial response to God's call reveal his doubts and insecurities? Have you ever felt inadequate when facing a significant challenge or decision?

4. Gideon asked for signs to confirm God's guidance. Why is it important to trust God's Word and not constantly seek signs or miracles in our own lives? What can excessive doubt and the need for signs indicate?

5. Consider God's decision to reduce Gideon's army to just 300 men. What might be the significance of this action? How does it illustrate the importance of relying on God's strength rather than our own in times of difficulty?

6. In what ways can Gideon's journey from fear to faith be applied to our own lives? How can we confront doubts and fears with trust in God's presence and promises?

7. Reflect on the idea that God often uses humble and unlikely individuals to accomplish His purposes. How can we recognize the potential for God's work in our own lives, even when we feel weak or inadequate?

8. How can we ensure that we give God the credit for our victories and successes, rather than attributing them solely to our own efforts?

9. Consider the concept of trusting in God's peace to face challenges boldly, as Gideon did. How can this trust in God's peace help us in our daily lives when confronting fears and uncertainties?

10. What practical steps can we take to apply the lessons from Gideon's story to our own faith journey? How can we move from fear and doubt to trust and obedience in our relationship with God?

Group Activity

Group Discussion: Divide into small groups and discuss a challenging situation or decision you currently face. What are your doubts and uncertainties? Together, brainstorm a few ways group participants can trust in God's guidance and overcome doubt.

Walking with God Today

Gideon's story teaches us that God can work through our doubts and weaknesses. Like Gideon, we may face moments of insecurity, but when we submit to God's call and trust in His strength, we can achieve victories for His glory. Remember that God often chooses the humble and unlikely to accomplish great things. Let us acknowledge His presence and power in our lives, even in times of uncertainty, and step forward in faith and obedience.

Lesson 10

A Woman Who Changed History: Hannah

Discovering the Power of Prayer

Read:
1 Samuel 1–3

Introduction

Hannah's story is found in 1 Samuel 1–3. She was the mother of Samuel, who became the greatest judge of Israel. Hannah was fervent in worship and had a very active prayer life. And her life is commendable for her willingness to follow through on a very costly commitment. Hannah's is an inspirational story on how God hears and answers prayer. We see how children are an incredible gift from God and how He is concerned for those who are oppressed and afflicted by wicked people.

Hannah, whose name means *grace,* was the favored wife of Elkanah. His other wife was Peninnah. Peninnah gave Elkanah sons and daughters, 1 Samuel 1.4, but Hannah was barren. The Lord had kept Hannah from conceiving, 1.5. Inability to bear children was a disgrace in Israelite culture. She would have been viewed as a failure and as a source of social embarrassment for her husband. Adding to this was the continual provoking of Peninnah, 1.6. The text does a good job letting us see her distress. She felt empty and useless because she could not produce an heir for her husband. Despite the best efforts of her husband, Hannah could not be consoled. Elkanah said:

> "Hannah, why are you crying?" her husband, Elkanah, would ask. "Why won't you eat? Why are you troubled? Am I not better to you than ten sons?" 1.8.

The events of 1.3-8 are set in the background of Elkanah's family going to Shiloh to offer up sacrifices to the Lord.

Hannah's Petition

When it came time for Hannah to present her offering, she entered the sanctuary weeping and knelt to entreat the Lord. She approached God humbly, referring to herself as God's "maidservant." In her prayer, she vows that if God would give her a son, she would dedicate him to the Lord and give him over for service to God all the days of his life.

While Hannah was praying, the high priest, Eli, sat on a chair observing her actions. As she prayed, she did so with her lips moving but no sound came out of her mouth. Eli spoke up and accused her of being drunk. It is tragic that this religious leader would automatically assume the worst of her. Hannah politely replies that she was not drunk, but that she was *pouring out her heart to the Lord,* 1.15. To this Eli replies, *go in peace, and may the God of Israel grant the request you've made of him,* 1.17.

After praying, she returned to her family and continued her meal. The Scripture says that her entire demeanor changed as "her face was no longer sad." After their visit to Shiloh, Elkanah and his family returned home.

There is great power in prayer! After making her petition, Hannah's change in attitude is notable.

- She honestly prayed to God, 1.11.
- She received encouragement from Eli, 1.17.
- She resolved to leave the problem with God, 1.18.

We should apply this formula in our prayer life today. Scripture assures us there is power in prayer:

- Matthew 7.7–8: *"Ask, and it will be given to you. Seek, and you will find. Knock, and the door will be opened to you. For everyone who asks receives, and the one who seeks finds, and to the one who knocks, the door will be opened.*
- Philippians 4.6–7: *Don't worry about anything, but in everything, through prayer and petition with thanksgiving, present your requests to God. And the peace of God, which surpasses all understanding, will guard your hearts and minds in Christ Jesus.*
- James 5.16: *Therefore, confess your sins to one another and pray for one another, so that you may be healed. The prayer of a righteous person is very powerful in its effect.*

Hannah's Prayer Answered

Soon afterward, Hannah conceived and gave birth to a son. The child was named Samuel, "name of God." The arrival of Samuel was a direct answer to Hannah's prayer in the sanctuary at Shiloh. The next year, Elkanah returned to the tabernacle to worship and pay his vow. Hannah did not accompany him, as she stayed at home until Samuel was weaned. Under Mosaic Law, women were not obligated to attend annual festivals. Smith has written, "Unless repudiated by her husband, the vow of a wife became an obligation upon her husband." What she had vowed concerning Samuel was now the responsibility of Elkanah.

Eastern women typically weaned their kids at the age of three years. After the weaning process, Hannah took a large offering and her son to the sanctuary at Shiloh. The family offered their sacrifice and brought the boy to Eli. She reminded Eli of her prayer that day three years earlier in the sanctuary. Samuel was the result of that prayer, and she would now give him to God for lifelong service. In response, Eli bows down in worship to the Lord.

The first eleven verses of chapter two contain a prayer of Hannah. In her prayer, God is the focus as she identifies four sources of great joy in her life.

1. She rejoiced for God answering her prayer in delivering her from the misery of being unable to bear children, 2.1.
2. She rejoiced in who God is. God is holy and possesses all strength and knowledge, 2.2–3.
3. She rejoiced in the reign and power of God. She expressed that over time, all things tend to work themselves out. God will make all things right, 2.4–8.
4. She rejoiced in her hope. She says that the righteous are always taken care of by God and the wicked are ultimately rejected, 2.9–10.

There is a Messianic prophecy in 2.10. The phrases, "strength to his king" and "exalt the horn of his anointed" refer to Jesus. After presenting Samuel to Eli, Hannah and the rest of Elkanah's family leave and return to Ramah. Samuel remained at Shiloh ministering to God under the supervision and training of Eli.

What's In This for Us?

Effective prayer calms the soul

Hannah carried a heavy burden each day knowing that she could not provide a child for her husband. The yearly trip to Shiloh and constant harassing by Peninnah only made matters worse. Things got so bad for Hannah that she could not eat. She decides to take the matter to God in prayer. Chapter 1:11 teaches that she completely opened her heart to God. She held nothing back. After Eli realized Hannah was praying and not drunk, he encouraged her by verbalizing his desire for God to grant her petition, 1.17.

Once Hannah opened her heart to God, she left the matter at His feet and trusted completely in Him. This is seen in how she returned to her family after prayer and was able to eat a meal. Now she was calm and resolute, knowing that the matter was in the hands of God. Prayer certainly brings peace. This is one of the greatest blessings of being a child of God. The result of Hannah's prayer? God heard and answered her prayer in a positive manner.

Don't let discouragement conquer you

Hannah had several things that could have contributed to her being down and having low self-esteem. She was unable to bear children. Her husband was in a relationship with another woman who constantly treated her with contempt. In human terms, her situation could not be changed. Elkanah was powerless to change her inability to bear children. After Hannah decided to take the matter to God, the high priest accused her of being drunk. She could have given up at that point. She did not. Instead, she continued and turned the matter over to God.

Don't be too quick to judge

Eli assumed Hannah was drunk when he saw Hannah praying. Instead of inquiring as to why Hannah was so emotional, Eli made a quick judgment and assumed the worst. Since we do not know what is in someone else's heart, we must guard against the danger of judging their heart and motives. Before we assume anything, we need to communicate and listen to them.

> "Do not look at his appearance or his stature because I have rejected him. Humans do not see what the LORD sees, for humans see what is visible, but the LORD sees the heart," 1 Samuel 16.7.

Follow through on your vows

When Hannah petitioned God, she made a deal with Him. She was not required to do so but did so anyway. When God answered her prayer, she followed through. How tough it must have been to leave her child with Eli in the sanctuary when the time came. When we make a vow to God, we must pay it.

Conclusion

During times of grief, discouragement, and persecution—we must turn to God for the answers. While we may not understand everything in this life, we know He cares for us and will never let us down. We must move in faith, trusting that God will work out solutions to life's problems.

And when God blesses us, we must be ready to express our thankfulness for all the ways He has blessed us. God is so good and will protect and provide for us as we go through life. As you look for Him, you'll be amazed to see how He has and is working in your life. What does He have planned for your future?

For Class Interaction and Discussion

Lesson Outline

1. **Hannah's Story from 1 Samuel 1–3:**

2. **Hannah's Petition:**

    —Her situation as a barren woman and the cultural significance.

    —Her distress was amplified due to Peninnah's provoking.

    —Her prayer in the sanctuary and the vow to dedicate a son to the Lord.

3. **Hannah's Prayer Answered:**

4. **Lessons for us:**

    —Effective prayer calms the soul

    —Don't allow discouragement to conquer you

    —Don't be too quick to judge

    —Follow through on your vows

Thought Questions for Discussion

1. Have you ever faced a situation that seemed insurmountable, like Hannah's inability to bear children? How did you deal with it?

2. How important is it to have a support system during times of distress, as Elkanah was to Hannah?

3. Discuss the significance of Hannah's humble approach to God in prayer. How can humility enhance our prayers?

4. Why do you think Eli initially misunderstood Hannah's actions as drunkenness? How can we avoid making hasty judgments about others?

5. Reflect on the power of prayer in Hannah's life. Have you experienced the transformative power of prayer in your own life? Share your experience.

6. How did Hannah's faith and commitment lead to the fulfillment of her prayer?

7. How did Hannah's prayer and commitment impact her relationship with God? What can we learn from her example in our own faith journeys?

8. How can prayer be a source of comfort and peace during challenging times?

9. Have you ever felt discouraged to the point of giving up? How did you overcome it?

10. Share instances when you or others were misjudged due to appearances or actions taken out of context. How can we avoid making assumptions about people?

Group Activity

Reflect and Commit: Divide into groups and discuss one area of life where you need to exercise more faith, prayer, commitment, or trust. Share your thoughts in small groups discussing strategies on how to apply these principles. Encourage each other to take the first step in improvement and share that with the group.

Walking with God Today

It is important that we turn to God in times of distress and experience the power of prayer. God is faithful and only through Him can we find real, genuine peace. Trust God with your burdens and look forward to the future with hope and confidence in His plans.

Lesson 11

A Man After God's Own Heart: David

Trusting God's Guidance in Life's Challenges

Read

Psalm 23

1 Samuel 17

Introduction

In Psalm 23, David took what people saw every day and caused them to see God. For the average person, nothing would have been more common than to see shepherds leading their sheep. The message of this Psalm would have immediately resonated in the mind of his readers as David skillfully painted a vivid image of the relationship he had with His heavenly Father. God was His Shepherd who fed, guided, and protected him.

David Followed with Absolute Trust

> Even when I go through the darkest valley, I fear no danger, for you are with me; your rod and your staff—they comfort me, 23.4.

It was extremely difficult to find water and pastures in the open range of the Middle East. Farmers grew grain in the green pastures, so sheep were forced to graze in areas where the grass was thin and scattered. As they dwelt in the wilderness, shepherds often found the best source of plentiful grass was in low, wet areas around a stream. These places were usually surrounded by high cliffs. It was the perfect situation for ambush. Wild animals often lurked in the shadows. When David speaks of the *dark valleys*, he thought of how some valleys could literally become the valley of death. Perhaps these were the areas where David had to defend both himself and his flock from predators, 1 Samuel 17.34–36a.

Sheep Trust the Shepherd

Sheep only went into these areas for one reason. They trusted the shepherd. The shepherd knew where he was going. Sheep followed because they trusted. When God is our shepherd, He will lead us through places we would not go without His leadership. He is the shepherd. We are His sheep. How much do we trust? There is a reason why David has been referred to as a man after God's heart, Acts 13.22. As we examine his life, we continually observe a life lived in complete trust and dependence on God.

For example,

- David trusted God in the incident with Goliath, 1 Samuel 17.
- Although not perfect by any means, David leaned on God during the years of Saul's persecution, 1 Samuel 20–30. See Psalm 18 for details on how David trusted in God during this difficult time.
- After being caught in grievous sin with Bathsheba, David threw himself on to the mercy of God, trusting in His forgiveness, Psalm 51.
- As David was forced to escape the royal city during the coup attempt by his son, Absalom, David depended on God, Psalm 3.

The Key to David's Success

David understood the key to his success. As He prepared his son Solomon to reign in his place he told him,

> As for you, Solomon my son, know the God of your father, and serve him wholeheartedly and with a willing mind, for the LORD searches every heart and understands the intention of every thought. If you seek him, he will be found by you, but if you abandon him, he will reject you forever, 1 Chronicles 28.9.

As we walk day by day with Christ, this can also be our source of success as well.

Every person in Christ must start at the same place: complete and total dependence on God. God has promised to be there for those who trust in Him. He is still working to fulfill those promises today and will continue to do so until the end of time.

The Physical World Can Cloud Our Spiritual Perspective

Sometimes it is very hard for us to see things from God's perspective. We live in a physical world. Our viewpoint is extremely limited. From where we stand, things can look daunting, depressing, and distressed. There are many things in our world that we cannot control. Who guides us through the valley? Who protects us while we navigate the path to greener pastures? We need someone more powerful than us. We need someone who can see things from a higher perspective. God is our Father, Deliverer, and Protector. God has promised:

> Keep your life free from the love of money. Be satisfied with what you have, for he himself has said, I will never leave you or abandon you. Therefore, we may boldly say, The Lord is my helper; I will not be afraid. What can man do to me? Hebrews 13.5–6.

Seeing Things from a Higher Perspective

God constantly challenges us to elevate our perspective and see things from a higher plane. Yet, our shortsightedness can cause us to view our circumstances mainly from an external perspective. This was certainly the problem behind Israel's fear and reluctance to fight Goliath. In the opening verses of 1 Samuel 17 the mighty warrior is described as a champion who stood over 9 feet tall. He had all the latest weaponry and would have had the strength and ability to use it effectively. No Israelite soldier believed they had the training and power to overcome. So, for over 40 days, they nervously stood on the sideline refusing to engage. There is no mention of anyone seeking God for guidance during this time. The silence is deafening. Saul's lack of faith and woefully inept demonstration of spiritual leadership are extremely visible here.

Then God's game-changer enters the scene. Sent on an errand by his father, David shows up on the front line never imagining how the day's events would turn out. Remember, he did not go there to fight. He simply went to deliver food to his brothers who were in the army of Saul. When he gets there, the troops were paralyzed with fear and refused to fight, 17.24. This was not the case with David. He was neither impressed with, nor intimidated by Goliath. David spoke to the men who were standing with him: *Just who is this uncircumcised Philistine that he should defy the armies of the living God,* 17.26. God was greater than anything Goliath could muster.

As the morning went by, David decided that Goliath could no longer be tolerated, 17.32. Saul tried to discourage him. David would not listen. With righteous anger he determined that he had to do this.

> Your servant has killed lions and bears; this uncircumcised Philistine will be like one of them, for he has defied the armies of the living God." Then David said, "The Lord who rescued me from the paw of the lion and the paw of the bear will rescue me from the hand of this

Philistine." Saul said to David, "Go, and may the Lord be with you, 17.36–37.

Because God had been there so many times for David, he knew it was imperative to involve God in the situation.

And so, David runs to the battle as Goliath mocks. What gave him so much confidence? He knew, beyond the shadow of a doubt, that God stood behind him! More important than any insult Goliath had hurled at Israel, Goliath had mocked the army of God. David knew God would never let this stand. This was the Lord's battle, 17.46.

The Lord's Battle

May we have the courage to see that the challenges we face today are the Lord's battles. God is our Father. He has personally invested in us and wants to see our ultimate good. Will we include Him in our struggles? Do we have the faith to put Him to the test? God can use any of our challenges as an opportunity to build our faith in Him. Do we have the confidence to confide in Him about everything? Will we trust Him to find a solution? Do we have the courage to always work according to His plans?

The trust we build in God grows over time. I love the writing found in Deuteronomy 7.21–26:

> Don't be terrified of them, for the Lord your God, a great and awesome God, is among you. The Lord your God will drive out these nations before you little by little. You will not be able to destroy them all at once; otherwise, the wild animals will become too numerous for you. The Lord your God will give them over to you and throw them into great confusion until they are destroyed. He will hand their kings over to you, and you will wipe out their names under heaven. No one will be able to stand against you; you will annihilate them. Burn up the carved images of their gods. Don't covet the silver and gold on the images and take it for yourself, or else you will be ensnared by it, for it is detestable to the Lord your God. Do not bring any detestable thing into your house, or you will be set apart for destruction like it. You are to abhor and detest it utterly because it is set apart for destruction.

Israel's conquests were not by their own strength, they were by the power of God. God told them He would clear away the nations "little by little." God could have cast out the inhabitants immediately and miraculously. Instead,

He chose to build Israel's faith and trust through time. With every challenge, God would provide the solution. They could live without fear because God would be with them all the way. Think of how these same promises have been made to God's sons and daughters today. Day by day we are being transformed into God's image. When the challenges of life confront us, we are not alone. As we struggle with our fleshly weaknesses, we are not alone. Little by little God works in our life, cleaning up our mess and making us new. We must not move in fear, but in faith and trust. God is actively working in your sanctification. When you give your heart to Him, He will stand behind you, protect you, and lead you to a better place.

> Now to him who is able to protect you from stumbling and to make you stand in the presence of his glory, without blemish and with great joy, Jude 24.

What's In This for Us?

Trust God's Leadership

Just as David trusted God as His shepherd, we should also trust God's guidance and leadership in our lives. Even in difficult and dangerous situations, our trust in God should remain unwavering.

Learning from David's Trust

We can learn from David's examples of trust in various challenging situations in his life, such as facing Goliath, enduring Saul's persecution, seeking God's forgiveness in times of sin, and depending on God during times of crisis like Absalom's coup attempt.

Complete Dependence on God

Our life with Christ requires complete and total dependence on God. Our success is rooted in knowing and serving God wholeheartedly. We must seek Him and trust in His promises.

Elevating Our Perspective

Our limited perspective in the physical world can sometimes lead to fear and discouragement. We should challenge ourselves to see things from God's higher perspective, just as David did when facing Goliath. Trusting in God's power can help us overcome daunting challenges.

God's Faithful Work in Our Lives

Like the Israelites who conquered nations "little by little" with God's help, we should recognize that God is actively working in our lives, guiding us, and transforming us day by day. We should not fear challenges but trust in God's ability to protect us and lead us to a better place as we strive for sanctification.

Conclusion

In conclusion, this lesson on Psalm 23 and the life of David provides us with insight into the importance of trust and complete dependence on God. Just as David entrusted his life to God as His Shepherd, we too should trust God's guidance, even when faced with the darkest valleys and challenges.

David's life serves as a remarkable example of consistently leaning on God in various circumstances, whether it was facing giants like Goliath, enduring persecution, seeking forgiveness, or navigating times of crisis. His unwavering trust in God is a great example for us.

Trusting in God's promises and seeking Him wholeheartedly are foundational to our success and growth as believers. We need to elevate our perspective, recognizing that our limited view of the physical world can sometimes lead to fear and discouragement. We are challenged to see things from God's higher perspective, trusting in His power to help us overcome daunting challenges.

Remember, God is actively at work in your life, just as He was with the Israelites who conquered nations "little by little." We should not be discouraged by the pace of our transformation but should trust that God is leading us to a better place through His guidance and protection.

For Class Interaction and Discussion

Lesson Outline
1. **David Followed in Absolute Trust:**

    —Sheep trust their shepherd

    —The key to David's success
2. **The Physical World Can Cloud Our Judgment:**

    — We need to see things from a higher perspective

    —Our battles are the Lord's, 1 Samuel 17.46

For Thought and Discussion

1. Share a personal experience where you had to trust God in a challenging situation. What did you learn from that experience?

2. Discuss the significance of David's trust in God in various episodes of his life, such as facing Goliath or enduring Saul's persecution. What lessons can we draw from his examples?

3. What does it mean to have complete and total dependence on God? How can we apply this principle in our daily lives?

4. Have you ever faced a situation where your limited perspective caused fear or discouragement? How can we strive to see things from God's higher perspective?

5. Share instances where you've seen God working in your life, gradually transforming you. How can recognizing God's faithfulness impact your faith?

Group Activities

Trust Building Exercise: Form pairs or small groups and share personal stories of trust in the Lord during challenging situations. Discuss how your faith played a role in those moments and what you learned.

Biblical Case Studies: Assign different biblical stories of trust and dependence on God to small groups. Have each group analyze the story and present key lessons to the class.

Sharing God's Faithfulness: Write down moments when you saw God at work in your life. Share these stories within the group as a source of encouragement.

Walking with God Today

Trust in God is the anchor that keeps you steady amidst life's storms. David's unwavering trust and dependence on God serve as a powerful example for every Christian. Your challenges may be daunting, but with faith, you can face them head-on, knowing that God is with you every step of the way.

Seek God wholeheartedly, elevate your perspective, and recognize His faithful work in your life. Challenges are not roadblocks but opportunities for your faith to grow. Keep moving forward with the assurance that God is leading you to a better place.

Lesson 12

Israel's Great Prophet: Elijah

Faith Lived Out

Read:
1 Kings 17–18

Introduction

We are first introduced to Elijah in 1 Kings 17. God raised him up to announce impending judgment over Israel. Over the previous fourteen years, Ahab and his wife Jezebel had been heavy proponents of Baal worship throughout the northern kingdom. Ahab (874–852 BC) was the son of Omri, who according to secular history was one of the more notable kings of Israel. He is mentioned in the annals of history in other nations at the time as a good trade partner. Omri and Ahab did much evil in the sight of the Lord, 1 Kings 16.25–33. His wife Jezebel was the daughter of the king of Sidon. Theirs was a marriage of political convenience as Israel valued Sidon as an important trade partner. But spiritually, the nation was dead. Ahab's window for self-judging and moving back toward God had passed.

God Brings a Drought on Israel

Throughout biblical history, God has given mankind time to repent before exacting judgment against them. See 1 Corinthians 11.31 and 2 Peter 3.9–10. God was now going to act against Israel by bringing in a severe famine in hopes of turning their hearts back to Him, 17.1.

Elijah's name means "Yahweh is my God." By promising a drought, this fell completely in line with God's warning about what would happen if His people forsook Him.

> Be careful that you are not enticed to turn aside, serve, and bow in worship to other gods. Then the LORD's anger will burn against you. He will shut the sky, and there will be no rain; the land will not yield its produce, and you will perish quickly from the good land the LORD is giving you, Deuteronomy 11.16–17.

See also Leviticus 26.18–19 and Deuteronomy 28.23–24.

The promise of a drought was God's direct challenge to Baal. Baal was a Phoenician god who was viewed as the storm god. Baal was also a fertility god. He was also known as the god of fire. Archaeologists have found depictions of Baal holding a thunderbolt in his hand. Baal worship included ritual prostitution, human sacrifice, as well as lascivious acts between male and female prostitutes. God hated Baal worship and considered it spiritual adultery. God used Elijah as a prophet to communicate His displeasure with His people.

Elijah's Time of Preparation—1 Kings 17

Journey to Cherith

Elijah's story is told primarily in 1 Kings 17–19. Chapter 17 may be viewed as a time of growth for Elijah. After communicating with Ahab in 17.1, God immediately sent Elijah to Cherith, which was east of the Jordan River. By sending Elijah here, God used this time (over two years, 18.1) as an opportunity to teach him that He would provide him with his needs. While Elijah was hidden away from Ahab, God built his faith and prepared him for what would happen on Mount Carmel. Through very personal experiences, Elijah would learn that God is the only source of life, fertility, and blessing.

God Alone Has Power Over Life

After dwelling in Cherith, where he was fed by ravens, God told him to go to Zarephath. Zarephath was in Phoenicia—the home of Baal worship. As these events occur, the drought is continually worsening. As Elijah approaches the village, he meets a widow who was gathering sticks to start a fire to cook her last meal. Widows would have been the first to run out of food during drought conditions, and there was no more way for her to provide for the needs of herself and her son. Elijah commanded her to give him water and prepare a meal for him. He promised that *the flour jar will not become empty and the oil jug will not run dry until the day the* LORD *sends rain on the surface of the land,* 17.14. Think of the message being communicated to the woman in this story. Here, in the homeland of Baal, the local god was powerless to provide for her most basic needs. God stands in unique contrast, who was more than able to care for the widow and her son.

Sometime later, the widow's son became very ill and died. Through the power of God, Elijah prayed and asked God to raise her son from the dead. 1 Kings 17.22 is the first restoration of a dead person recorded in Scripture.

Throughout 17.17–24 we see the intimate relationship Elijah had with God. His heartfelt prayer, 17.21, was heard and answered by God, 17.22. Throughout this process, Elijah was learning about the great power of God as well as the power of prayer. God was communicating to the widow as well as Elijah that He alone has power over life—not Baal.

Elijah on Mount Carmel—1 Kings 18

The Mission

At the beginning of 1 Kings 18, the drought was inside its third year. It was especially severe in Samaria, most likely because Ahab and Jezebel lived there. Elijah, who had been dwelling in Zarephath, was told to go down to meet Ahab. His mission is spelled out in 18.19 as he told Ahab to *summon all Israel to meet me at Mount Carmel, along with the 450 prophets of Baal and the 400 prophets of Asherah who eat at Jezebel's table.* Mount Carmel was located geographically between Israel and Phoenicia and was regarded as Baal's sacred dwelling place. The mountain often was shrouded in clouds and had many storms filled with lighting and thunder. The ancients believed this was a sign that deity dwelt there. Mount Carmel was regarded as "the garden land" and was famous for its fertility.

The scene described in 18.17–40 is most certainly dramatic. Elijah stands as one against the 450 prophets of Baal. Probably hundreds, if not thousands, gathered since he summoned all Israel to Mount Carmel. In the minds of many, Baal would have had a distinct advantage in this contest. Elijah knew that this victory would require a supernatural act of God. He moves forward in faith—publicly challenging the prophets.

> "Then you call on the name of your god, and I will call on the name of the LORD. The God who answers with fire, he is God." All the people answered, "That's fine," 1 Kings 18.24.

The prophets of Baal did as Elijah instructed and for six hours, they cried out…to no avail. As they did, Elijah mocked them, 18.27. By doing this, Elijah was exposing Baal's limited power.

The Victory

Finally, at the time of the afternoon sacrifice, Elijah called the people to him and rebuilt the altar of the Lord. When all was ready, he prayed a prayer for God's glory:

"LORD, the God of Abraham, Isaac, and Israel, today let it be known that you are God in Israel and I am your servant, and that at your word I have done all these things. Answer me, LORD! Answer me so that this people will know that you, the LORD, are God and that you have turned their hearts back," 1 Kings 18.36–37.

God immediately revealed Himself. The Israelites turned back to God and demonstrated repentance through their obedience to the Law by killing the false prophets, 18.40.

What's In This for Us?

There are times of life where God prepares us to carry out His plan

Elijah's experiences in chapter 17 were difficult at best. God called him to stand up to Ahab, announce judgment, and then depart into the wilderness. Elijah immediately responded. As he descends into the wilderness east of the Jordan, he has taken no personal provisions. As the drought worsens, his personal circumstances would have been very stressful. Yet, God used this time in his life to teach him to rely on Him. Not even the ravens feed their young, but God commanded them to feed Elijah. Day by day they brought him food. Elijah took his water by the nearby brook, until the lengthy drought caused it to dry up.

This would have been a time of great patience by Elijah—trusting in God for the very basics of life. As you endure difficult circumstances and times of trial in your life, view the situation as an opportunity for God to strengthen and establish your faith. God will work through various means to teach us dependence on Him. How much do we trust? Had Elijah not gone through the times of difficult training in 1 Kings 17, he may not have been prepared to serve as he did in chapter 18.

We must make a decision

1 Kings 18 identifies the problem Israel had. Elijah asked the people,

> Then Elijah approached all the people and said, "How long will you waver between two opinions? If the LORD is God, follow him. But if Baal, follow him." But the people didn't answer him a word, 1 Kings 18.21.

At issue in this story is not so much that Israel wanted to reject Yahweh and choose Baal, as it was they wanted to serve both Baal and Yahweh. Elijah calls for an either/or decision. Isn't the same necessary for us? We have been called to be decisive and choose God.

> "No one can serve two masters, since either he will hate one and love the other, or he will be devoted to one and despise the other. You cannot serve both God and money, Matthew 6.24.

Yet we often struggle. Too many have difficulty with leaving worldly desires behind and wholeheartedly committing to Christ. There are several Scriptures which urge us to follow through:

- **Luke 9.57–62**—"No one who puts his hand to the plow and looks back is fit for the kingdom of God," 9.62.
- **James 4.4**—You adulterous people! Don't you know that friendship with the world is hostility toward God? So, whoever wants to be the friend of the world becomes the enemy of God.
- **2 Corinthians 6.1–2**—Working together with him, we also appeal to you, "Don't receive the grace of God in vain." For he says: At an acceptable time I listened to you, and in the day of salvation I helped you. See, now is the acceptable time; now is the day of salvation!

Finally, our lack of decisiveness is an indication of lukewarmness, of which the Lord is very displeased, Revelation 3.16–18.

We must walk in faith and obedience, just like Elijah

Elijah proved his faith in God by living it out. While the situation he faced may have been fraught with fear, he responded with tremendous trust. Every time we move forward in faith—God will stand behind us. We will reap wonderful rewards. To those who live by faith, eternal life is promised:

> Be faithful to the point of death, and I will give you the crown of life, Revelation 2.10b.

> You see that a person is justified by works and not by faith alone. In the same way, wasn't Rahab the prostitute also justified by works in receiving the messengers and sending them out by a different route? For just as the body without the spirit is dead, so also faith without works is dead, James 2.24–26.

Conclusion

God often prepares us for His divine plan through times of difficulty and testing. Elijah's experiences in the wilderness taught him dependence on God, even for the most basic provisions. Likewise, in our own lives, challenges and trials can be opportunities for God to strengthen our faith, molding us into vessels ready for His service, James 1.1–8.

Elijah's bold challenge on Mount Carmel also teaches us the importance of making a decisive choice. Israel wavered between serving God and Baal, but Elijah called for a clear decision. Similarly, we must choose wholeheartedly to follow God, leaving behind worldly desires and distractions. Lukewarmness is displeasing to the Lord, and we are called to be resolute in our commitment to Him.

The promise of eternal life awaits those who remain faithful, and our faith must be accompanied by actions that demonstrate our commitment to God. Just as the body without the spirit is dead, faith without works is lifeless. Let us, therefore, be faithful to the point of death and strive to receive the crown of life that awaits those who walk in faith.

For Class Interaction and Discussion

Lesson Outline

1. **God's Time of Preparation for Elijah, 1 Kings 17:**

    —Journey to Cherith

    —God alone has power over life

2. **Elijah's Time on Mt. Carmel, 1 Kings 18:**

    —The mission

    —The victory

3. **What's in this for us?**

    —We will have to endure seasons of preparation

    —We must choose God

    —We must walk in faith and obedience just like Elijah

For Thought and Discussion

1. What were the circumstances in Israel that led to God's call for Elijah to announce judgment and a drought? How does this reflect the consequences of spiritual unfaithfulness?

2. What can we learn from Elijah's experiences in Cherith and Zarephath about dependence on God during challenging times? How does God use difficulties to prepare us for His purpose?

3. What significance did Mount Carmel hold in the contest between God and Baal? How did Elijah's unwavering faith in God lead to the people's repentance and return to God?

4. How does Elijah's challenge to Israel resonate with our own need for decisiveness in following God? What worldly distractions do we need to leave behind to wholeheartedly commit to Him?

5. *Living Out Our Faith:* What actions and behaviors exemplified Elijah's faith? How can we ensure that our faith is not merely words but is demonstrated through our actions and obedience?

Group Activities

1. *Elijah's Wilderness Experience:* Divide into small groups and discuss a personal experience where you felt God was preparing you during a challenging time. Share how it strengthened your faith.
2. *Mount Carmel Revisited:* Discuss Elijah's encounter with the prophets of Baal on Mount Carmel. Talk about the significance of God's response and the people's repentance. How can we apply this lesson to our lives today?
3. *Making Decisive Choices:* In pairs, identify areas in your life where you need to make more decisive choices in your commitment to God. Share your goals and support each other in taking action.
4. *Living Out Your Faith:* Share personal examples of how your faith has been demonstrated through your actions. Discuss how faith and works are interconnected in your daily life.

Walking with God Today

Faith, testing, and obedience are integral parts of our faith. Just as Elijah faced daunting challenges and remained obedient to God's calling, we too must navigate life's trials with unwavering faith.

Trust in God's preparation during challenging times, make decisive choices to follow Him, and let your faith shine through your actions. Elijah's story reminds us that God is with us every step of the way.

Lesson 13

For a Time Like This: Esther

Trusting in God's Providence

Read

The Book of Esther

Introduction

The story of Esther is set during the Persian Empire's reign in the 5th century BC. It is a time when the Jewish people were living in exile, having been taken captive by the Babylonians and later released under Persian rule. The Persian King Ahasuerus (also known as Xerxes I) ruled over a vast empire, stretching from India to Ethiopia.

The principal characters in the story are Esther, the Jewish orphan who becomes queen of Persia. Mordecai is Esther's cousin and guardian, a wise and faithful Jewish man. King Ahasuerus (Xerxes I) is the Persian king who chooses Esther as his queen. Haman is the king's wicked advisor who plots to annihilate the Jewish people. And finally, there is the Jewish people, the chosen ones of God living in exile, who face imminent danger.

The Story

The book of Esther is a unique and powerful narrative within the biblical canon, rich with themes of providence, courage, and the survival of the Jewish people in the face of adversity.

Chapter 1 begins with a lavish banquet hosted by King Ahasuerus, during which Queen Vashti is banished for her refusal to appear before the king and his guests. This leads to a kingdom-wide search for a new queen, a search that brings Esther, a Jewish orphan raised by her cousin Mordecai, into the spotlight, 2.1–14. Esther finds favor in the king's eyes, but she keeps her Jewish identity hidden. In the background, Mordecai uncovers and foils a plot to assassinate the king, a deed that is recorded in the royal records but initially goes unrewarded, 2.21–23.

The plot thickens with the rise of Haman, the king's advisor, who harbors a deep hatred for Mordecai and the Jewish people. When Mordecai refuses to bow to Haman, Haman's anger leads to a decree to exterminate all Jews in the empire, 3.1–11. Unaware of Esther's Jewish identity, King Ahasuerus endorses Haman's plan, setting a date for this catastrophic event. Mordecai, upon learning of this decree, turns to Esther, urging her to reveal her identity to the king and plead for her people. Chapter 4.14 contains probably the most well-known verse in the book:

> If you keep silent at this time, relief and deliverance will come to the Jewish people from another place, but you and your father's family will be destroyed. Who knows, perhaps you have come to your royal position for such a time as this."

Esther's response is one of brave resolve. She organizes a fast among the Jewish community and prepares to approach the king unsummoned, an act punishable by death. In a dramatic turn of events, Esther reveals her Jewish identity to King Ahasuerus during a banquet and exposes Haman's plot, 7.1–6. The king, furious at Haman's deceit, orders his execution, 7.7–10.

The story concludes with a twist of divine justice and irony. Though the king's decree against the Jews cannot be revoked, he issues a new decree allowing the Jews to defend themselves, 8.9–14. Led by Mordecai, now honored by the king, the Jewish people triumph over their adversaries, 9.1–17. The events lead to the establishment of the festival of Purim, a celebration of Jewish survival and deliverance, as recorded in the closing chapters of the book, 9.26–32.

The Book of Esther, while not directly mentioning God, showcases the themes of providence, courage, and faith in the face of overwhelming odds. It serves as a reminder of the resilience and faith of the Jewish people, and the mysterious ways in which deliverance can come in times of peril.

What's In This for Us?

God's Providence

The Book of Esther is filled with instances of providence and hidden guidance. This characteristic of the story invites us to recognize God's hand at work even in situations where His presence isn't overtly acknowledged or visible.

> A person's heart plans his way, but the LORD determines his steps, Proverbs 16.9.

In Esther's story, we see a series of 'coincidences' or events that align in a way that ultimately leads to the deliverance of the Jewish people. From Esther's ascension to the throne to Mordecai's timely discovery of the assassination plot, and even the king's sleepless night leading to the reading of the chronicles, each event contributes to the salvation of the Jews. We need to look for and trust in God's providence in our own lives, understanding that He may be working behind the scenes in ways we cannot immediately comprehend.

> We know that all things work together for the good of those who love God, who are called according to his purpose, Romans 8.28.

Courage in Adversity

Esther's courage in risking her life to save her people exemplifies faith in action, a faith that operates even when the path forward is unclear or perilous. This reflects the idea that recognizing God's providential hand often requires a leap of faith, a trust in His ultimate goodness and plans, even when they are not fully understood. God's plans are often beyond human understanding, *"For my thoughts are not your thoughts, and your ways are not my ways." This is the Lord's declaration. "For as heaven is higher than earth, so my ways are higher than your ways, and my thoughts than your thoughts,* Isaiah 55.8–9. We trust that God is always at work in our lives, even in times of seeming absence or silence. But they are always purposeful. Faith looks beyond immediate circumstances and trusts in God's overarching plan and providence.

> Never let loyalty and faithfulness leave you. Tie them around your neck; write them on the tablet of your heart. Then you will find favor and high regard with God and people. Trust in the Lord with all your heart, and do not rely on your own understanding; in all your ways know him, and he will make your paths straight, Proverbs 3.3–6.

> Now faith is the reality of what is hoped for, the proof of what is not seen, Hebrews 11.1

Faithful Friends

Mordecai's role in Esther's life goes beyond kinship; he is her guide, protector, and most importantly, a faithful friend. His unwavering support is evident in how he nurtures and raises Esther after she is orphaned, advises her wisely when she becomes queen, and even risks his own safety to ensure her well-being and that of their people. This level of commitment and loyalty in a friendship is rare and invaluable.

Who are the 'Mordecais' in your life—those individuals who stand by you through various seasons, offering guidance, support, and unwavering loyalty? These are friends who don't necessarily share the limelight with you but are instrumental in our growth and success. They are our confidantes, our mentors, and our anchors, often believing in us more than we believe in ourselves.

We need to appreciate these individuals more deeply, recognizing that their support is a critical component of our life. Just as Mordecai's wisdom and dedication were pivotal in Esther's journey, so too are the contributions of those who guide and support us in our personal and professional lives.

> Oil and incense bring joy to the heart, and the sweetness of a friend is better than self-counsel, Proverbs 27.9.

We should also consider the qualities that make such friendships enduring and impactful. It points to virtues like loyalty, selflessness, wisdom, and the willingness to speak the truth and offer guidance even when it's difficult.

> The wounds of a friend are trustworthy, but the kisses of an enemy are excessive, Proverbs 27.6.

Mordecai, for example, doesn't shy away from urging Esther to step into a dangerous role for the greater good, exemplifying how true friends challenge us to grow and step beyond our comfort zones.

> Two are better than one because they have a good reward for their efforts. For if either falls, his companion can lift him up; but pity the one who falls without another to lift him up, Ecclesiastes 4.9–10.

The Danger of Pride

Haman, elevated to a high position by King Ahasuerus, becomes consumed with pride and arrogance. His sense of self-importance is so inflated that he expects everyone to bow to him. Pride can distort one's perspective, leading to disproportionately destructive responses to personal slights. Haman's pride blinded him to reason, leading to decisions that are not only morally reprehensible but also ultimately self-destructive.

> Pride comes before destruction, and an arrogant spirit before a fall, Proverbs 16.18.

Haman's fate—a demise brought about by his own schemes—underscores the biblical wisdom that pride often precedes a fall. It's a vivid illustration of how personal vendettas and prideful ambition can lead to one's undoing.

> When arrogance comes, disgrace follows, but with humility comes wisdom, Proverbs 11.2

> But he gives greater grace. Therefore he says: God resists the proud but gives grace to the humble, James 4.6.

We must recognize the potential dangers of allowing pride to dominate our actions and decisions. When pride takes precedence over humility and respect for others, it sets us on a path that not only harms those around us but also leads to our own downfall.

> In the same way, you who are younger, be subject to the elders. All of you clothe yourselves with humility toward one another, because God resists the proud but gives grace to the humble, 1 Peter 5.5.

God Uses Ordinary People

Throughout Scripture we discover ordinary, seemingly unremarkable individuals are often chosen by God to fulfill significant roles and achieve great deeds. Esther's story is a prime example of this concept. As an orphan and a member of a minority group in exile, she would have been viewed by many in her society as insignificant or powerless. Yet, it is precisely this 'ordinary' young woman who is elevated to the position of queen and becomes instrumental in saving her people. Hers is a powerful testament to the idea that one's humble beginnings or societal status do not limit God's ability to effect change or bring greatness.

God often chooses the least likely individuals to carry out His will. This choice serves multiple purposes:

1. It highlights the power and wisdom of God (in contrast to human expectations and standards).
2. It illustrates that everyone has the potential to be an agent of significant change.
3. It serves as a reminder that societal status or wealth does not equate to favor in the eyes of God.

Zooming out, each of us needs to see the potential for divine purpose in our life, regardless of our background or current circumstances. Faith calls us to remain open to the possibility that we, too, could be used for significant purposes, often in ways we might not expect.

he has toppled the mighty from their thrones and exalted the lowly, Luke 1.52.

It also serves as a reminder of the value and potential inherent in every person, challenging common ideas that might otherwise dismiss certain people as 'ordinary' or 'insignificant.' In Esther's story we discover potential, divine purpose, and the extraordinary possibilities that can arise from the most ordinary beginnings.

But many who are first will be last, and the last first, Matthew 19.30.

Conclusion

Esther's remarkable journey from obscurity to a position of influence and the deliverance of her people highlights this truth: God's purposes prevail through the lives of those who may seem least likely to bear such weighty roles. Esther's story is a call to all Christians to live with a sense of divine purpose, recognizing that we personally, regardless of our beginnings or status, have the potential to be used by God in ways that surpass our imagination, Ephesians 3.20–21. This story challenges us to be attentive to the workings of providence in our lives, to respond with courage when called upon, and to stand firm in faith even when the path ahead is shrouded in uncertainty, Hebrews 11.1.

The virtues of Esther and Mordecai—courage, faithfulness, wisdom—are values we need. We also need to be aware of the danger of pride like Haman's. Our world often celebrates the self-exalted and overlooks the humble. The book of Esther offers a counter-narrative, elevating the ordinary for God's extraordinary purposes. Every act of faith and every moment of courage can make a real difference, just as Esther's did. We are, each one of us, positioned "for such a time as this" to impact the world in our unique ways, guided by the hand of a powerful God.

For Class Interaction and Discussion

Lesson Outline

1. The Story:
2. What's in This for Us?

    —God's providence

    —Courage in adversity

    —Faithful friends

    —The danger of pride

    —God uses ordinary people

Thought Questions for Discussion

1. How do you see the theme of divine providence at play in the story of Esther, and how does it encourage you to look for God's hand in your own life?

2. In what ways does the character of Esther inspire you to act courageously in your personal life, especially when faced with difficult decisions?

3. Mordecai's guidance to Esther was pivotal. How important is it to have mentors like Mordecai in our lives, and how can we be that for others?

4. The Book of Esther never explicitly mentions God, yet His presence is felt throughout. How does this shape your understanding of how God can work through circumstances, even when He seems silent?

5. Haman's downfall was a result of his pride. Can you think of a time when pride led to negative consequences in your life or the life of someone you know?

6. Esther's story involved significant risk for the greater good. Discuss a time when you had to take a risk for what you believed was right. What was the outcome?

7. Reflect on the cultural and societal barriers Esther faced. How can her story empower us to overcome similar challenges in our own society today?

8. The festival of Purim was established to remember the Jews' deliverance. Why is it important to commemorate and remember the ways in which we have seen deliverance and victory in our lives or community?

Group Activities

Character Study: Have each group focus on a character from the Book of Esther (e.g., Esther, Mordecai, Haman, King Ahasuerus) and prepare a short presentation on their character's role, motivations, and lessons that can be learned from their actions.

Providence Mapping: Have participants reflect on their own lives and identify moments of providence or 'hidden guidance.' They can map these out on paper, creating a visual representation of how they see God's hand at work in their own story.

Walking with God Today

You have been placed in your current positions for a divine purpose. Like Esther, you may feel ordinary, but within you lies the potential for extraordinary impact. You are called for such a time as this, equipped and empowered to act boldly for the good of others, guided by wisdom and supported by faith. Remember, the same God who orchestrated Esther's life is active in your life, weaving together a narrative of grace, redemption, and purpose.